Reinventing Your Life After Retirement

Defining Your Best Life with
Confidence and Purpose;
New Ventures, Body & Brain
Health, Financial Well-Being,
Social Ties, Guided Downsizing

Every Day is a Saturday!

by
Sallie Wright Abbas

TABLE OF CONTENTS

Introduction

Don't deny the dreams. They're a gift given to make your life full. Accept them. Reach for them. We are here to live, to serve, to trust, and to create out of our longings. — Jane Kirkpatrick

Imagine waking up on the first day of your retirement. You no longer have to set an alarm clock, dress up for work, or sit in rush hour traffic. It feels like summer vacation, but it's for the rest of your life instead of just a few weeks. You have a new reality, and the possibilities are endless. You have a 64-color box of crayons and can design the rest of your life. But with this new reality comes an unstructured time and, for some, a loss of identity. Embrace the wide-open possibilities and intentionally create the life you've always imagined. It's never too late to enrich your life with wisdom, grace, humor, and new ventures.

As you approach your retirement age or maybe have just stepped across that threshold, you may be experiencing many emotions. It's not uncommon to feel anxious, worried, or even depressed as you contemplate the changes that are coming your way. You may be wondering what your purpose will be once you're no longer working or how you'll fill your days without the structure of a job to guide you.

You may have worked for the same company for many years and have built your identity around your job title. Retirement can feel like you're losing a part of yourself, leaving you feeling lost and unsure of who you are without your work.

Furthermore, you may feel like you're running out of time to accomplish your dreams and goals. You may feel like your best years are behind you, and you're left with regrets about what you didn't do or achieve.

Dreams don't die because you get older; you get old because your dreams die.

It's understandable to feel overwhelmed by these thoughts and emotions. Retirement is a significant life transition, and it's natural to feel discomfort as you navigate this new chapter.

This book is here to say that retirement doesn't have to be the end of your purpose or your dreams. It's an opportunity to explore new possibilities and pursue the things that bring you joy and fulfillment. Retirement can be a time of great growth, learning, and fun with the right mindset and approach.

You have a new reality. Retirement is like having summer vacation from school that lasts all year. ...Endless vacation! Celebrate: no commute, no alarm clock!

I know that retirement can be an incredibly fulfilling and rewarding chapter of life. It can be a time to pursue new passions, connect with loved ones, and positively impact the world.

This book will guide you on this journey and help you create a rich and satisfying life after 60.

Most importantly, I have deep empathy and compassion for those going through this journey. I know retirement can be a time of great uncertainty and vulnerability, and I am committed to providing guidance and support to struggling people.

You are likely searching for clarifying the new meaning in your life, your *raison d'etre*, as the French say --one's reason for being or waking each morning joyfully. You are likely reading this book seeking some help to find your motivating purpose in life. There is a term, **ikigai** in Japanese, that gives guidance to finding this path. Consider this diagram; it helps to define the goal of this search.

Your **passion** is a combination or intersection of **what you love** and **what you are good at**.

What you love and **what the world needs** intersect to define your mission.

What the world needs and **what you can get paid for** intersect to become your **vocation**.

And at the intersection of **what you are good at** and **what you can get paid for** is your *profession*.

Where they all come together is that almost magical center –your *ikigai*.

A sense of fulfillment comes from being devoted to what one loves, aiming at mastery and accomplishment. It is a continuing journey that also brings great satisfaction.

You have the freedom to create your best life. We make our own meaning in life.

Reading this book will provide you with a wealth of knowledge and insights into how to enrich your life after 60. You will gain a deeper understanding of the challenges and opportunities that come with retirement, and you'll learn practical strategies for navigating this new chapter of your life.

One of the main benefits of reading this book is that it will help you shift your mindset from fear and uncertainty to possibility and excitement. You'll learn how to approach retirement as a time of growth and exploration rather than an end to your purpose or dreams. By adopting a positive and proactive attitude, you'll be better equipped to make the most of this new chapter in your life.

This book will also provide practical guidance on setting goals and staying focused on what's most important to you. You'll learn how to prioritize your time and energy to pursue the activities and experiences that bring you the most joy and fulfillment.

In addition, this book will offer valuable insights into maintaining your physical, mental, and emotional health as you age. You'll learn about the importance of exercise, nutrition, and social connections, as well as strategies for managing stress and maintaining a positive outlook on life.

Another benefit of reading this book is that it will provide you with inspiration and motivation to keep learning and growing. You'll discover new hobbies, interests, and passions you may not have had the time or opportunity to explore. You'll also learn about new career opportunities, volunteer work, and other ways to stay engaged and active in your community.

Reading this book will help you approach retirement with excitement and possibility rather than fear and uncertainty. You'll gain valuable insights, practical strategies, and inspiration to help you create a rich and fulfilling life after 60.

Reinventing Your Life After Retirement is not just a collection of tips and strategies but a roadmap to help you define your life on your terms. This book will inspire you to dream big and take action. With practical advice, inspiring stories, and a deep understanding of the unique challenges and opportunities of retirement, ***Reinventing Your Life After Retirement*** will empower you to live the life you've imagined. So why wait? Take the leap and start living your best life today!

> 1 <
Setting Goals

"I learned this, at least, by my experiment: that if one advances confidently in the direction of his dreams and endeavors to live the life which he has imagined, he will meet with a success unexpected in common hours." — Henry David Thoreau, *Walden: Or, Life in the Woods*

 The secret to success is setting goals and consistently taking action toward them. How do you know what your goals should be? Pause to consider what it means for your life after retirement. Consider some of your interests, skills, or personal values. What do you want to do with the rest of your life?[1]

Are you looking to be more social or help in the community? Are you interested in traveling or being around your family more? What are your hobbies, such as cooking, reading, gardening, or something else? What are some of your interests in life that you're passionate about?

There is no better time than now to set and achieve new goals. Do you have a vision for the future of your life? If

---

[1] "Get inspired to live your best life" from United Health Care AARP

not, it might be about time for some self-reflection and goal-setting.

The role of goals in success is that it is easier to accomplish a goal once you know what you want to accomplish. Goals clearly outline what you want to achieve, how you will get there. Goals are essential in determining an individual's direction, talent, commitment, and time needed to reach goals.

Goal setting is possible if you can identify the many opportunities available to you. Goal setting can motivate you to take on challenges you may not have thought you could handle.

Types of goals:
• Short-term goals include such things as drinking more water daily, improving your diet, pursuing a passion project, taking up a hobby, etc.

• Long-term goals may require significant effort to achieve and months, years, or even decades in the future. Some examples: are financial stability, becoming a better spouse or married couple, increasing your emotional intelligence, learning a new skill, etc.

• Financial goals focus on your financial situation. These are goals that you can set for extended outcomes. Some examples: eliminating debt, saving more money, etc.

You are more likely to get what you want if you have specific objectives. Most people don't know how to define their life goals, so they concentrate on the small parts and lose sight of the big picture.

You are now more in control than ever of what you want your outcomes to be. You may need to focus on what is important to you. You can make a goal more real by working towards it. This helps keep it alive and motivates you to achieve this goal. If you do pursue them and don't achieve them, it will still help to work toward them to develop a clearer vision of your future. If you have a goal in sight, it will make it more likely for you incorporate anything new that comes your way.

Decide how to define the years ahead.

Don't be afraid to set high standards for your future. After you've achieved a goal, you can set a new one. Be bold on your goals; set the stage for success in the future!

Picture yourself living a successful life. You are freed from day-to-day pressures and have a guiding overview of your life. Decide how to define the years ahead. This will also allow you to appreciate every moment of your journey toward them.

You are a new you. Defining is a challenge. What does your life look like? Probably it is not as organized as a map, but perhaps it can take the form of a to-do list.

The process of planning and visualizing how your ideal life will function is not a linear one. You start off thinking it would be cool to live out of a van in a forest, then realize you don't want to lose your relationship with your community.. It's not that the things you want to accomplish are too difficult; it's just that they are too big!

Here are some potential scenarios to help you in getting started. Perhaps you would like to:

- Be generous with more than money, your time, and your skill. Be generous and positive.
- Use your energy to help people, listen and give them some of your best.
- Give more than you take.
- Build great relationships with others, particularly those who have the same values as yours.
- Be with people who support your goals, cheer you on, and help you work towards them. Build a solid relationship with parents, siblings, or other close family members to help motivate success.

A plan for refining your goals

1. Identify the qualities in the scenarios you generate that would make your ideal life happen. Refer to the list beginning on page 6.
2. Begin cultivating those very same qualities right now. Here's an exercise to help you begin:
   - Write down a list of these qualities and rank them from most important to least important.
   - Once you've generated this list, write on some index cards the top three. You could achieve all the qualities you listed to live the ideal life at some point in your life. Each goal will lead you closer to living your dream life and help prepare you for it.

- List the qualities you want to deepen or cultivate-- one per card.
- Randomly draw a quality card at the start of your day.
- Throughout that day, focus on that single quality. Notice where it's present and where it's absent. Consider how it might change an encounter, a plan, or a task. Implement that quality all day long, every way you can.
- Write on that card any insights you gained regarding that particular quality.

Once the goal is broken down into small goals, you are more likely to achieve them. It is rewarding to see how you are moving ahead. Picture how great it will feel when you achieve your goal. As long as you are moving toward your desired outcome, it is only a matter of time before what you want is yours.

Visualize your world once you have attained your objectives. What will it feel like when you've achieved these goals?

Each goal can have multiple outcomes, but you may only achieve some. However, make holding onto your objectives into a lifestyle. Each objective will deliver new enjoyable and tough experiences, but each will provide additional motivation and strength to get the job done (achievements). Your world will be richer and more colorful than you first envisioned.

Set one or two objectives at a time. Don't overwhelm yourself by setting too many objectives at once.

The key to success is to be realistic. Set small, attainable objectives, and strive to achieve them. This will help keep you motivated as you embark on this new phase of your life. You'll soon be on the way to your ultimate objective!

Imagine the life you want to enjoy. Picture how you would navigate your ordinary days and describe the world you want to live in and how you will get there. Work out a list of goals that will take you from where you are now to where you want to be. Your work defining your image can help guide your choices as you strive for the life you've imagined.

After you've laid out your goals to plan for that "new you," arrange to try out what you hope to do.

For instance, you might choose to wake up early, exercise regularly, and eat a healthy diet. Now break down what it would take to attain each of these qualities. If you are going to wake up early and exercise regularly, your plan must also address how you will manage the rest of your day if you get sleepy or hungry.

Scientific research has shown that goal setting can promote both physical and mental health outcomes, such as increased self-esteem and improved quality of life, by increasing positive emotion states (e.g., hope). This is achieved by imagining the positive outcomes should you reach your goal(s) and writing down any obstacles that could get in your way.

So, break down your goals into bite-size pieces and work in increments rather than trying to achieve everything all at once. Your life doesn't need to be perfect.

Consider this list of qualities you may like to emphasize and cultivate:

Acceptance	Compassion	Experimentation
Accountability	Competence	Exhilaration
Achievement	Confidence	Exploration
Adaptability	Consciousness	Fairness
Adventure	Consistency	Faith
Affection	Contentment	Family
Altruism	Cooperation	Fearlessness
Ambition	Courage	Flexibility
Authenticity	Courtesy	Forgiveness
Awareness	Creativity	Freedom
Balance	Curiosity	Friendliness
Beauty	Decisiveness	Fun
Bravery	Dedication	Generosity
Calmness	Dependability	Gentleness
Candor	Determination	Giving
Capability	Discipline	Grace
Care	Diversity	Gratitude
Challenge	Drive	Growth
Charity	Empathy	Happiness
Cleanliness	Encouragement	Harmony
Clear-mindedness	Energy	Health
Collaboration	Enthusiasm	Helpfulness
Comfort	Excellence	Honesty
Commitment	Excitement	Honor

Hope	Mastery	Productivity
Humility	Maturity	Professionalism
Humor	Meaning	Prosperity
Imagination	Mindfulness	Punctuality
Improvement	Modesty	Purpose
Independence	Motivation	Rationality
Industry	Nurturing	Realism
Influence	Open-mindedness	Reassurance
Initiative	Optimism	Recognition
Innovation	Order	Recreation
Insight	Originality	Reflection
Inspiration	Passion	Reliability
Integrity	Patience	Resilience
Intelligence	Peace	Respect
Intensity	Perfection	Responsibility
Intimacy	Perseverance	Restraint
Introspection	Persistence	Reverence
Inventiveness	Personal	Risk-taking
Joy	Expression	Sacrifice
Justice	Playfulness	Security
Kindness	Pleasure	Self-control
Knowledge	Positivity	Selflessness
Leadership	Potential	Self-reliance
Learning	Power	Self-Respect
Liberty	Pragmatism	Sensitivity
Light-heartedness	Precision	Serenity
Love	Preparedness	Service
Loyalty	Presence	Sharing

Simplicity	Temperance	Valor
Sincerity	Tenacity	Variety
Solidarity	Thankfulness	Vitality
Spirituality	Thoroughness	Warmth
Spontaneity	Thoughtfulness	Wealth
Stability	Tolerance	Willingness
Strength	Tranquility	Winning
Success	Trust	Wisdom
Support	Trustworthiness	Vigor
Sustainability	Truthfulness	Vision
Sympathy	Understanding	Versatility
Tact	Uniqueness	
Teamwork	Unity	

Seeing Possibilities:

An attitude of gratitude keeps your outlook positive and is an important component of overall well-being. A positive attitude gives a person more energy, and they are happier and healthier than those with negative attitudes.

A positive attitude can make a huge difference in your life. A positive attitude helps you appreciate and enjoy the good things you have instead of grumbling about the bad things you don't have. A good attitude towards life can help you see possibilities and opportunities rather than problems and difficulties.

Remembering your goals daily will keep you on track to achieving them, whatever they are.

Find something meaningful to accomplish in setting a goal: A goal that is meaningful to you will make your life more productive and enjoyable. For the goal to be meaningful, it has to mean something to you.

Feed your passion: Passion leads to action, and it is much easier to accomplish things when you are passionate about them.

Be flexible: Your goals may change because you learn new things about yourself and your goals. If this happens, don't give up; tweak your goal and make your goal achievable for you.

Your health and fitness are important because they should be part of your life and goals.

Goal setting assists in maintaining focus; other things will distract you and might cause you to lose sight of your goals. Don't give up after a few days or weeks of trying.

Two specific goals I am setting for myself are:

_____

_____

> 2 <
A Healthy You, Setting new health practices:

"Take care of your body. It's the only place you have to live in." — Jim Rohn.

To have a healthy body, it's crucial not just to do things that are good for you but also to make choices about the things that aren't. For example, eating well and exercising regularly is necessary for a healthy life. Avoiding bad habits such as smoking or drinking excessively is also essential.

Changing your lifestyle in these ways can be challenging at first, but like anything else, it takes some time to feel normal. Eventually, you find that you no longer need willpower every time you're tempted by something unhealthy because your habits will have changed. If you are starting a new routine and feeling anxious over whether it will be enough to change your life, try not to think about it too much. Just start doing it and see how you feel afterward. Of course, before beginning any new health program, you'll want to consult with your physician to make sure it's safe for you.

As you begin creating the healthiest version of yourself, consider the changes you make as habits rather than short-term goals. Like with any other habit, once you exercise or eat well every day, it will eventually become part of your routine.

Start small and work your way up. You might begin your journey to a healthy life by exercising for 10 minutes a day. As you are able, increase the intensity of your workout. Take it from being an intentional program to being a habit. Building a habit takes time, but soon it can be part of your new reality.

Care for your skin and teeth:

Protect your skin from the sun. Sun exposure can cause wrinkles and other skin problems, leading to more severe conditions like cancer. Avoid tanning booths because they have been linked with cancer.

Using a mild scrub or cream to help cleanse your skin is better than soap. You can also make your face look smoother by using an exfoliating mask to remove dead skin cells or a gentle scrub to soften the surface of your skin. Moisturizing daily protects your skin and improves your looks. Yes, you men, too.

Wearing a hat with brim is a great idea for protecting your facial skin.

Healthy food can also help to reduce wrinkles and make your skin look younger. More about that in Chapter 3.

Brushing twice daily with a toothbrush that is neither too soft nor too hard will remove plaque from the teeth that can lead to cavities and bad breath. (You may hear your mother's voice echoing in your ear!) Combine that with daily flossing to further improve plaque removal and prevent decay. A water flossing machine is very effective, too. And finally, a helpful little tool is the interdental brush (a tiny brush that can go between the teeth and remove even more plaque than floss!). Removing bacteria from the mouth is serious business!

There are 11 main bacteria that cause gum disease. If left untreated these bacteria can destroy gum tissue and bone and cause tooth loss. These bacteria also get into our bloodstream and can cause systemic problems in heart, joints, brain, etc.

Interestingly enough, only one type of bacteria is responsible for causing cavities, Streptococcus Mutans.

You probably know that tobacco smoke and alcohol may harm the tooth enamel, as does letting sugar linger in the mouth.

Staying hydrated is vital as it helps maintain your skin and also flushes out microbes from your body. Do you drink the recommended amount of water per day? You've probably heard the advice that you should drink eight glasses of water a day. That's a reasonable goal. Most healthy people can stay hydrated by drinking water and other fluids whenever they feel thirsty. For some people, fewer than eight glasses a day might be enough. But other people might need more, for example, if they spend time outside or exercise heavily. Water intake makes it possible to flush out your system and prevent disease from affecting it. Eating juicy fresh fruit like an orange in the morning will increase your metabolism and help you lose weight effectively. Drinking a big glass of water before lunch or dinner will fill you up before eating a main meal, so that you don't overeat. Many people drink water or other beverage <u>with</u> the meal; some authorities say that water <u>before</u> the meal may be better, as it doesn't dilute the digestive process.

Benefits from Exercise

Exercise is excellent for general physical health and for brain health — helping people problem-solve, think, sleep better, and boost their energy and spirits. An exercise program needs to exercise the musculoskeletal system and move all muscles and joints. Importantly, however, every exercise program needs to start with a visit to your primary care provider, who will take into account your current fitness level, cardiovascular health, weight, and other factors to counsel you on the advisability of your preferred program.

Exercise increases blood flow, which eases stress, which in turn reduces wrinkles!

Maintaining or regaining muscles of younger years – exercise program

You can increase or regain the lost muscle mass that comes with age by using the proper exercise and diet. Many experts believe resistance and weight training are the best ways to rebuild muscle. In addition to increasing muscle mass, this form of exercise increases bone mass, another critical factor in staying mobile as you age. Begin with a gentler activity, such as water aerobics, light dumbbells, or stretch band exercises, and gradually increase the weight and repetitions (reps).

Exercise:– Your max heart rate can be calculated from 220 minus your age. With vigorous exercise, you should aim for 70%- 85% of this max.

Finding a fitness technique:

A fitness technique is performing an exercise to target specific muscle groups. Physical fitness extends life, prevents chronic disease, and is one of the most effective strategies for improving mental health. Exercise on a regular basis can lower your chances of developing heart disease, hypertension, stroke, type 2 diabetes, and colon and breast cancer. It can have a significant favorable impact in reducing depression, anxiety, and stress. It can improve memory, sleep, and your general mood.

Your plan should fit your life. You can do it at home, 20 min per day. Use a trigger reminder: connect it with another habit or daily occurrence: brush your teeth, take a morning medicine, feed the dog, make your coffee or tea, check e-mail, afternoon arrival at home.

Work out three times a week for 30 minutes to an hour. This will increase your stamina and help you look in shape.

The best way to get the most out of your workout is to try various techniques. An appropriate one will:

• Increasing muscle definition
• Improve performance in sports and other high-intensity activities
• Prevent joint pain
• Prevent or reverse osteoporosis
• Reduce chronic aches or pains.

Selecting a fitness technique involves identifying the muscles you want to target and the exercises you want to use.

The three basic types of exercise are Weight-bearing exercise (hiking, playing pickleball, dancing), Resistance exercise (strength training), and Balance exercises (preventing falls).

Exercises That Boost Strength and Balance:

You'll see your balance and strength improve by including exercises that boost both. Strength-building exercises include push-ups, triceps dips, pull-ups, and the one-handed overhead press. A good way to improve your balance is to work on your core. Exercises for the core include planks, sit-ups, bridges, and leg raises. Walking, biking, and climbing stairs strengthen muscles in your lower body. A recumbent bike or stair stepper is a safe way to start if your balance needs a lot of work.

The type of exercises you do, your food choices, and the right way to exercise are all necessary. If you work hard and put in a little effort each day, you will look and feel great.

Maintaining or regaining muscle mass can be a challenge for many older adults. This happens because our muscles don't get as much blood flow as younger people's muscles do because of our age-related declines in circulation. Have a reminder note where you'll see it, especially the 21-60 days to establish the habit. No excuses, but if you go without doing it one day, don't beat yourself up. Select a set number of repetitions and sets for each exercise.

Gentle Exercises

Sit-To-Stand

Length of exercise: 30 seconds Total time: 5 minutes; Areas worked on: abdominals, back, glutes, quadriceps, hamstrings

Directions:

1. Sit in a chair with your feet flat on the floor and about hip-width apart. The feet should be slightly behind the knees for leverage.
2. Slowly stand up and remain standing for 10 seconds as you regain balance. Use your hands and arms if needed. Return to a seated position.
3. Repeat 10 times.
4. To level up: Hold a five-pound weight between your hands while you do this exercise for added resistance.
5. Take note: Going from a sitting to a standing position is a daily skill that is needed. Ensure that the chair you use in

this exercise is sturdy and will not move as you sit, stand, and return to sit.

Toe Raises

Length of exercise: 15 seconds - Total time: 2 minutes 30 seconds - Areas worked on: calves, feet. Calf muscle strength is important for ankle stability.

Directions:

1. Sit in a chair with your feet flat on the floor. Place your hands on the tops of your thighs.

2. Slowly raise your toes off the floor. You may notice your upper body wanting to lean back but stay upright and slightly lean forward if you need to. Hold for 10 seconds, then lower toes back down.

3. Repeat 10 times.

4. To level up: Alternate between raising toes and raising heels.

5. Take note: If your calf muscles start to burn, take a rest between repetitions.

Trunk Circles

Length of exercise: 2 minutes; Total time: 6 minutes; Areas worked on: abdominals, obliques, lower back

Directions:

1. Sit in a chair with your feet flat on the floor and hip-width apart. Place your hands on top of your thighs.

2. Keep the lower body stationary while you move your shoulders and torso forward, right, back, and left in a clockwise motion. Make 10 big circles. Switch directions

and move shoulders and torso forward, left, back, and right in a counter-clockwise motion for 10 circles.

3. Repeat two more times in each direction.

4. To level up: Hold your arms straight out from your sides while doing the exercise.

5. Take note: This exercise helps train the body in weight shifts and directional changes. Keep your eyes focused on a stationary object straight in front of you for added balance.

Three-Way Hip Kick

Length of exercise: 30 seconds; Total time: 5 minutes; Areas worked on: abdominals, hips

Directions:

1. Stand up tall with your feet about hip-width apart. Place hands on the back of a chair or on a countertop.

2. Extend your right foot and point it out in front of you. Return to the original position. Now extend the right foot out to the right side and then return. Finally, extend the right foot to the back and then return. If the floor was a clock, your right foot would point toward the 12, the 3, and the 6 o'clock positions.

3. Switch legs and now extend the left foot to the front, the left, and the back. Your right foot would point towards the 12, the 9, and the 6 o'clock positions.

4. Repeat 10 times on each leg.

5. Take note: Strength in the hip muscles is important for walking, changing direction, and going up and down

stairs. Take care not to arch your lower back while completing this exercise.

After working out for a month, you can celebrate the achievement and also check yourself out in the mirror. Check for improved posture: level shoulders? Torso straight (no forward or backward lean)? Chin over toes? A straight line from the center of the forehead to the midpoint between feet? Is the neck not curving forward? Celebrate your change at the one-month mark!

Higher-Energy Exercises

Try these for more stamina, muscle building, energy

Seated Leg Taps

Length of exercise: 30 seconds Total time: 5 minutes Areas worked on: abdominals, hip flexors, quadriceps

Directions:

1. Sit up tall in a chair with your knees bent and feet flat on the floor. Place your hands on the sides of the seat for support.

2. Tighten your abdominal muscles and straighten both legs out in front of you, lifting both feet off the floor. Try to bring the legs parallel to the floor. Slowly lower your right foot and tap the floor. Bring it back up. Slowly lower your left foot and tap the floor. Bring it back up.

3. Continue alternating tapping the right foot and then the left.

4. Repeat 10 times.

5. To level up: To make it more challenging, raise and lower both feet at the same time.

Take note: If you need to take a break, lower both feet to the floor for a quick rest before repeating the exercise.

Seated Side Bends

Length of exercise: 1 minute; Total time: 5 minutes; Areas worked on: abdominals, obliques

Directions:

1. Sit up tall in a chair with your knees bent and feet flat on the floor. Arms should be hanging at your sides.

2. Bend and raise your right arm, placing your right hand gently on the side of your head while looking straight ahead. Bend at the waist and lean your upper body to the left. Extend your left hand down towards the floor as far as you can as you continue looking straight ahead. Slowly come back up to the starting position. Repeat 10 times.

3. Switch sides and raise your left arm, placing your left hand on the side of your head. Extend your right hand down towards the floor as you bend at the waist and lean to the right. Remember to keep looking straight ahead. Come back up to the starting position. Repeat 10 times.

4. Rest, then repeat the exercise one more time on both sides.

5. To level up: Straighten your bent arm above your head as you lean your body to the side.

6. Pay attention to your neck and shoulders. Don't hunch up. Keep your shoulders down and away from your ears.

Superman

Length of exercise: 30 seconds; Total time: 5 minutes; Areas worked on: abdominals, upper back, lower back, hip flexors, glutes.

Directions:

1. Lie on the floor or a padded mat, facing down. Extend your arms out straight over your head and legs straight out behind you. Your body should form a straight line.

2. Tighten the abdominal muscles as you lift your hands and feet off the floor. Keep your neck neutral and gaze looking at the floor. (This will help to avoid straining your neck .)Hold the lifted position for 10 seconds, then slowly lower back down to the ground.

3. Repeat 10 times.

Burpees are a great multi-muscle exercise activity, but if you haven't exercised in a while don't start with this one! They combine jump, squat, plank, and push-up into one. It's not easy, but it is effective! See the videos at

https://www.youtube.com/watch?v=qLBImHhCXSw   or
https://www.youtube.com/watch?v=tJrdJBWBuo8

Burpees:

Exercise routines and workouts

Aging Backwards Fast Track - Miranda Esmonde-White
pp. 108-345; good easy-to-follow illustrations

Young for Life –– Marilyn Diamond & Dr. Donald Schnell
Practice balance, posture, and flexibility

Other types of exercise, non-traditional

- Yoga is a system of stretching and positional exercises originating in ancient India to promote good health, fitness, and control of the mind.

- Tai Chi: Taiji (advanced takes longer to learn) vs. Qigong (simpler, beginner) - connecting mind, body spirit.
  Benefits: cardiovascular, respiratory, gastrointestinal, harmonize body chemistry, improve metabolism, prevent brain aging and memory loss.

- Zumba - a fitness program that involves cardio and Latin-inspired dance. It's great in a group, live, but you can also find some Zumba classes online, especially YouTube.

- International Folkdance - traditional dances from many countries; with the varied styles and music of countries as diverse as Bulgaria, France, England, Poland, Romania, Russia. You may be able to find a local group.

More about yoga

Yoga has many benefits as we age. Yoga can help to keep us mobile and more flexible, and even more focused.

Yoga can increase strength in the core back muscles, decreasing back pain and correcting posture.

As we age, if we are not continuing to stay mobile and keep our bodies moving, we can easily begin to lose our flexibility; practicing yoga promotes flexibility. This, in turn, helps with mobility and staying active.

As the years go by, you might find that you experience more pain. It may be due to arthritis, tendonitis and tendinopathy, loss of muscle fibers, a decrease in flexibility, tightening of the fascia, etc. When doing yoga, the body can be stretched out and tight areas can be released. In addition, yoga helps to drain toxins from the body, and some poses even help to drain the lymph nodes, leading to less inflammation. As a result, yoga can help with chronic pain.

Yoga can improve cardiorespiratory fitness by decreasing stress and lowering blood pressure and heart rate.

In getting older, our balance often decreases. Yoga involves many balancing poses. Even if you cannot fully do a pose, there are always modifications that you can do to practice with a bit of support, building your balance up over time.
bodybyyoga.training/yoga-for-men/yoga-for-men-over-50/

Best Yoga Poses for Older Adults
www.forbes.com/health/healthy-aging/best-yoga-poses-for-older-adults/

Balance

Balance exercises are especially important because they can help you prevent falls and maintain your independence. It's a great idea to include balance training along with other physical activity.

- Try walking in a line, heel to toe, for a short distance.

- While standing, balance on one foot. Can you put on a sock while standing on the other foot?

- Other balance exercises:

https://stayingsharp.aarp.org/activities/improve-balance-health/
https://www.mayoclinic.org/healthy-lifestyle/fitness/multimedia/balance-exercises/sls-20076853?s=4

https://www.mayoclinic.org/healthy-lifestyle/fitness/multimedia/balance-exercises/sls-20076853?s=2

Healthy Weight

Exercise and good eating habits make for a healthy weight. What's a healthy weight? Check the online Body Mass Index calculator - a tool to tell you if you are underweight, a healthy weight, overweight, or obese based on your body mass index.

https://www.aarp.org/health/healthy-living/info-2017/bmi_calculator.html

The types of exercises I think would suit me best are:

_____

> **3** <
Food Awareness:

"Let food be thy medicine." – Hypocrites

"Came From a Plant, Eat It; Was Made In a Plant, Don't." – Michael Pollan, Author, and Journalist

Good habits in what we eat.

Today's problem is that so many of us are entirely unaware of what we eat, which means we could easily consume too much or not get enough nutrition to keep our bodies in shape. Life can be hectic at times,  but taking the time to become more food aware, along with some education, could mean the difference between being fit and healthy and being sick and sad.

One easy way to make a new habit stick is by making it something or part of a routine you already do all the time. Eating breakfast is your daily fuel, so why not add more fruit and veggies? Make this an easy commitment by choosing foods already in your refrigerator or pantry, so there's no extra effort to eat healthily.

If there are foods that you are buying that you know aren't supportive of your goals, think about ways to alter them or choose healthier versions. For example, if you love bagels, buy whole wheat instead! l.

It is best to eat nutrient-dense meals and eat at least five to six times daily. Three small meals per day won't keep you healthy. A breakfast is recommended. This will jump-start your metabolism and set you up for a great day. However, this may be overridden if you decide to engage in intermittent fasting. (See p. 42)

It's also important to remember that eating healthy is not about skipping meals or starving yourself. It's about eating regularly and ensuring that your food is nutrient-dense and energy-promoting.

We can become overweight, underweight, and at risk of developing diseases and conditions such as arthritis, diabetes, and heart disease if we consume too much food or food that gives our bodies the wrong instructions.

Reducing heart disease, stroke, and diabetes are primary health goals to be accomplished through diet (that is, eating good foods) and physical exercise.

The nutrients in our food allow our cells to fulfill their essential activities. Consider it like growing a garden. For the best results when planting tomato seeds, utilize the proper soil and sunlight. But, if you use poor dirt and don't give it enough sunlight, you might get a tomato, but it might not be the ripest, roundest, reddest, or tastiest tomato.

Other than potatoes, corn, and peas, you can eat as much as you want of almost any vegetable. A cup of chopped broccoli or a grilled portobello mushroom contains just 30 calories and less than 1 gram of fat. Two entire cups of lettuce yield less than 16 calories. A whole tomato has just 22 calories because of its high-water content. Other vegetables that are also nutrient-dense and light in calories are cauliflower, kale, carrots, and sprouts.

What makes them so beneficial for weight maintenance and weight loss is that they are high in macronutrients [such as carbohydrates] and micronutrients [vitamins and minerals], as well as rich in fiber. Fiber keeps blood sugar levels stable, helping you avoid sudden attacks of the "munchies" when otherwise you might crave junk foods.

Ten foods you can eat without getting fat.

1. Celery
2. Lettuce
3. Watermelon
4. Broccoli and cauliflower
5. Grapefruit
6. Mushrooms
7. Berries (strawberries, blueberries, blackberries)
8. Kiwi
9. Carrots
10. Spinach and kale

If you're not a fan of vegetables, try these to make your veggies more palatable:

- Roast them in olive oil spray, then add garlic, other herbs, and spices,

- Dip can be high in fat, so use salsa instead (adding even more vegetables!)

- Blend a ranch-dressing flavor packet into plain yogurt (preferably Greek yogurt), and that adds protein!

When nutrition intake does not regularly match the basic needs of cell activity, metabolic activities slow down or even cease.

Some foods and their effects:

Water: Water is a significant part of the body. It is used in many processes and everyday activities. The body loses and gains water all day, so it is essential to drink lots of water daily (or get some form of hydration), whether it's tea, lemonade, or water itself.

<u>Salt</u>: Salt has several purposes in the body. It helps with the nervous system, balances fluids and minerals, aids digestion, and even regulates blood pressure. However, too much salt can cause health problems such as heart disease and hypertension.

<u>Sugar</u>: Sugars provide energy for the body, and the brain uses sugar as energy. However, too much sugar can cause problems with weight and health.

Fruit: Fruits contain vitamins and nutrients that help keep the body healthy. Fresh fruit is good for your palate, and frozen or dried fruit is easy to take on long hikes or travels. Certain fruits, like avocados, are high in fat and calories, but contain healthy monounsaturated fats, Vitamins B, C, E, K, folate, potassium, magnesium & carotenoids.[2] And others, like bananas, can be quickly digested.

<u>Fiber</u> is a vital diet component because it helps prevent constipation, keeps blood sugars stable, and assists in hormone regulation.

Vitamins and other supplements:

While food and water are necessary for the body to operate optimally, they aren't always enough. In some cases, extra nutrients, such as vitamins and minerals, may be required to maintain health. If a person is following a ketogenic diet or any other low-carbohydrate diet, then it is likely that additional supplementation will be necessary to replenish any deficiencies.

---

[2] https://www.hsph.harvard.edu/nutritionsource/avocados/

When the body does not receive enough carbohydrates from the digestive tract, it breaks down fats in the liver. This produces ketones which can then be used as energy instead of carbohydrates. The liver becomes fatigued after about twenty hours without readily available carbohydrates (such as those in grains). [3]

Some of the essential vitamins in your body are:

• Vitamin A: For skin, hair, eyes, and teeth. It also helps to boost the immune system and helps with cell growth. Key sources of vitamin A are the following vegetables: carrots, dark green leafy veggies, sweet potatoes, mangos, etc. T This vitamin can be found in animal sources as well as some oils.

• Vitamin B: Not just one, but a group of vitamins involved in converting food into energy (carbs) and other body fuels (fat and protein). The B vitamins help with memory and mood, reduce the risk of heart disease, boost the immune system to ward off infection, reduce inflammation, reduce the risk of anemia (a lack of red blood cells), and help maintain a healthy metabolism. There are eight different types of B vitamins, including thiamine (B1), riboflavin (B2), niacin (B3), vitamin B5 (pantothenic acid), vitamin B6, biotin (B7), folate and folic acid and vitamin B12.

• Vitamin C: Helps the body produce collagen, which helps with the growth of bones, dental health, and wound healing. It also aids in fighting off infection and reducing inflammation in the body. Though this is a water-soluble

---

[3] https://www.ncbi.nlm.nih.gov/pmc/articles/PMC7008768/

vitamin, it can be stored in some areas of the body for long periods. Vitamin C can be found in some fruits and vegetables, and in tiny amounts in some animal sources. According to the National Institutes of Health, citrus fruits, tomatoes and tomato juice, and potatoes are major contributors of vitamin C to the American diet. Other good food sources include red and green peppers, kiwifruit, broccoli, strawberries, Brussels sprouts, and cantaloupe.[4]
It also stops scurvy. We must all be getting at least a basic amount because who has heard of scurvy lately?

• Vitamin D: Aids in the absorption of calcium and phosphorus to produce new bones, teeth, and tissues. It also helps with the regulation of hormones and healthy blood clotting.

• Vitamin E: Helps to reduce inflammation in the body, helps prevent damage to cells caused by free radicals, and boosts the immune system. This vitamin can be found in some foods, including whole grains (wheat germ), nuts (almonds, walnuts), and seeds (sunflower seeds).

• Vitamin K: Assists in blood clotting and calcium absorption. This vitamin can be found in leafy green vegetables such as kale, cabbage, spinach, and collard greens.

• Vitamin H, also known as B7 (Biotin): Helps to convert carbohydrates into energy. Biotin can be found in egg yolks, milk, nuts, legumes, and some cereals. If you are eating healthy foods in your diet, eating less junk and sugary and fatty foods, adding vitamin supplements may not be necessary.

---

[4] ods.od.nih.gov/factsheets/VitaminC-HealthProfessional/

Cucumbers contain most of the vitamins you need every day, just one cucumber contains Vitamin B1, Vitamin B2, Vitamin B3, Vitamin B5, Vitamin B6, Folic Acid, Vitamin C, Calcium, Iron, Magnesium, Phosphorus, Potassium and Zinc.

Good carbohydrates:

Carbohydrate-rich foods are a crucial component of a balanced diet. The body receives glucose from carbohydrates, which is then transformed into energy for maintaining biological processes and engaging in physical activity. However, the quality of the carbohydrates is crucial, and some foods high in carbohydrates are superior to others.

The healthiest sources of carbohydrates—unprocessed or minimally processed whole grains, vegetables, fruits, and beans—promote good health by delivering vitamins, minerals, fiber, and a host of important phytonutrients.

• Folic acid/folate: Used for the growth of new cells and synthesis of DNA. It also helps with the regulation of hormones and healthy blood clotting. Folate helps with erythrocyte (red blood cell) production and inhibits anemia (a lack of red blood cells).

What to avoid in your diet:

• Fast-acting carbohydrates: These foods can lead to high blood sugar levels, which cause insulin resistance and diabetes over time. This can quickly lead to weight gain in a short amount of time if you aren't careful. Apple sauce, soda, candy bars, and cookies are some examples of fast-acting foods you should avoid most of the time.

• High-fat foods: You should limit the unhealthy fats you consume, including meat, butter, oils, cheese, ice cream; the body cannot digest them well due to their high fat content and can clog up the digestive tract, leading to weight gain. Fat calories are stored as fat in the body; overeating this type of food will cause weight gain and may eventually lead to health problems (see Obesity). Nuts, seeds, and avocados, are also high calorie, but with monounsaturated fat, and so should be eaten in moderation.

• It's easy to know why to avoid or at least limit: candy, ice cream, and doughnuts. The answer is SUGAR! Sugar is an isolated simple carbohydrate with no nutritional value. It contains four calories per gram, compared with fat which has nine calories per gram.

Awareness of how much sugar has been added to a food product can be seen by checking the back label of the product or directly referring to the nutrition facts on the food label. If any ingredients end in "ose" (dextrose, fructose, lactose, glucose), that food is most likely also high in sugar and, therefore, should be avoided.

Artificial sweeteners: Artificial sweeteners are common in many processed foods, including sugar-free candies and soft drinks. However, these can cause damage to the body in several ways: they disrupt gut bacteria, cause insulin resistance, and stimulate the appetite for sweets and calories, among other things. Natural sweeteners such as honey and dates are acceptable on their own but probably should not be added to anything that is not naturally sweetened (such as a salad).

The label shown here is one among the few brands of ketchup that have no high fructose corn syrup. High fructose corn syrup is a highly processed sweetener derived from corn. Like other sugars, it is relatively harmless when eaten in its source food but disease-causing after extraction. It is cheap, plentiful, and shelf-stable, making it a ubiquitous ingredient in processed foods. Avoid it when you can!

Fructose consumption has increased significantly because of the extensive use of HFCS in beverages and processed foods. This sweetener has also been shown to cause negative health effects, especially diabetes.

• Alcohol: It can easily alter the respiratory rate, breathing patterns, and heart rate. This can lead to insomnia and should be avoided.

Why is the Mediterranean diet considered to be the best choice for a healthy body (especially the heart), and a Keto diet not? A ketogenic diet has numerous risks. Topping these is that it's high in saturated fat. A recommendation is that you keep saturated fats to no more than 7% of your daily calories because of the link to heart disease.

In contrast, the foundation of the Mediterranean diet consists of minimally processed plant-based foods, such as whole grains, vegetables (including potatoes), legumes, fruits, nuts, seeds, herbs, and spices. Olive oil is the main source of added fat in the Mediterranean diet, which includes dairy products, eggs, fish, and poultry in low to moderate amounts; they are more common than red meat in this diet. Wine may be consumed in low to moderate amounts, usually with meals. Fruit is a common dessert instead of sweets.

• Say "No" to hot dogs. Why should these be avoided? They contain sodium nitrate, a common preservative used in cured meat products, including bacon, deli meat, and jerky (also the related additive sodium nitrite). It has been linked to the development of diabetes and heart disease. These concerns have led to food processors cutting out these additives from some foods, but not all.

• Caffeine: Caffeine is a stimulant and worsens the effects of a low-carbohydrate diet. However, it is still possible to be on a low-carbohydrate diet and consume some caffeine.

• Artificial sweeteners, flavors, and additives: These products are artificial, can cause damage to the gut lining, disrupt the gut bacteria and cause insulin resistance.

• Foods with gluten/grains: Grains contain gluten, which is problematic for many who suffer from leaky gut syndrome.

The whole grain has enough fiber that, if eaten in moderation, shouldn't cause any problems. Persons with celiac disease could experience life-threatening problems from ingesting gluten.

One study found those who drank beverages sweetened with high fructose corn syrup or sugar daily for only two weeks developed insulin resistance. Researchers have also found insulin resistance to be a critical risk factor for dementia, leading many experts to call Alzheimer's disease "Type 3 diabetes" [The Epoch Times March 22-28, 2023 p.C3]

The truth about cholesterol

Cholesterol is a natural component in everyone's blood and supports functions within the body. It's only when bad cholesterol causes plaque to build up in your arteries that it's considered a major risk factor for heart attack, heart disease, and stroke.

Regarding good and bad cholesterol: Your liver produces cholesterol! It is found in every cell in your body. It stabilizes the cell walls.

There are 2 types of cholesterol:

LDL (low-density lipoprotein) cholesterol is often called the "bad" cholesterol because it collects in the walls of your blood vessels, raising your chances of health problems like a heart attack or stroke. However, your body needs some LDL to protect its nerves and make healthy cells and hormones. It also helps repair cells and arteries. It is delivered to where it is needed.

HDL (high-density lipoprotein) cholesterol, sometimes called "good" cholesterol, absorbs cholesterol in the blood and carries it back to the liver. The liver then flushes it from the body. High levels of HDL cholesterol can lower your risk for heart disease and stroke.

Have you heard LDL = bad and HDL = good? Now you know: they work in balance.

Your Weight

Gaining weight as you get older isn't inevitable. Our bodies change as we enter our late 30s and early 40s, and those changes accelerate toward 50. And several things happen to our bodies that most weight management programs don't consider because most diet plans are developed and marketed to people in their 20s and 30s, and early 40s.

Straightforward tweaks to how we eat could set us on the path to maintaining and building muscle and keeping weight off. Our metabolisms don't slow in mid-life, not until at least age 60.

So, the fact that we gain weight as we age and seem to have more difficulty burning calories or keeping weight off is not because of metabolism as we once thought.

Don't try to lose weight just by reducing calories; Severely restricting the calories you eat sends your body a message that it needs to prepare for a time of famine, which automatically reduces the number of calories your body burns while you're resting — including sitting at the computer and watching TV. Ultra-low-calorie diets can <u>sabotage</u> your efforts to lose weight.

The solution is to eat better (the good foods, the right foods!), exercise more, and manage stress. The changes you make to your weight will significantly impact your health; it's also important to understand that slow and steady wins the race.

Muscle building may be one of the most overlooked aspects of a weight loss or strength training program. But it is one of the most critical bumps in someone's physical transformation. Techniques used in muscle-building programs are usually compound, where many muscles are worked out simultaneously.

You will love being so healthy and active in these post-retirement years!

Many people are unaware that consuming the right carbs to lose weight is extremely important. Carbohydrates are essential for weight loss because they help <u>burn fat</u> so you stay fit and look beautiful.

See Chapter 5 on ways to "feed" your brain.

Intermittent Fasting

More people are now aware of the concept of intermittent fasting.

Intermittent fasting (IF) is an efficient method of balancing the body's use of food, and good cells survive a fast; old cells may not survive a fast; the body then uses stem cells to produce good new cells.

Intermittent fasting is a dietary plan in which one cycles between periods of eating and periods of fasting. The goal is to increase the body's sensitivity to insulin, reduce inflammation, and promote cell repair.

Here are several types of intermittent fasting. Some may involve a daily schedule, alternate days, or twice weekly:

16/8 Method: Fast for 16 hours and eat within an 8-hour window. Many people skip breakfast and have their first meal around noon, then finish their last meal before 8 pm.

5-2 Diet: This involves eating normally for 5 days of the week and then restricting calories to 500-600 for the remaining 2 days. These days don't need to be consecutive, and people can choose whichever days they prefer to fast.

Eat-Stop-Eat: Fast for 24 hours once or twice a week. Perhaps you might normally eat on Tuesday and Thursday but then fast after Tuesday dinner starting the fast at 8 pm to Wednesday dinner at 8 pm.

Alternate-Day Fasting: Alternate between normal eating and fasting on alternate days. On fasting days, you might eat one small meal of around 500 calories.

One Meal a Day (OMAD): Eat only one meal a day, usually choosing a one-hour window each day. This meal should be nutrient-dense; make sure you get all the necessary nutrients for the day.

It's important to note that IF is not suitable for everyone, especially those with medical conditions or pregnant or breastfeeding. You definitely should talk to a healthcare professional before starting any new dietary practice.

Food affects mood

The foods we eat not only affect our mood but our sleep patterns and our energy levels," says psychologist Susan Albers, PsyD. "And that can impact us throughout the entire day."

Here are a few ways in which your diet can influence your mood:

The food you eat can affect your blood sugar levels, which in turn can impact your mood. When your blood sugar levels are low, you may feel tired, irritable, or anxious. When your blood sugar levels are stable, you may feel more energized and alert.

Brain chemicals: Certain foods can affect the production of neurotransmitters in your brain, such as serotonin and dopamine, and both are linked to mood regulation. Consuming foods that are rich in tryptophan, such as turkey, can boost serotonin levels and improve your mood. Feel good after Thanksgiving dinner? Maybe you can credit the turkey!

Your gut health plays a significant role in overall health, your sense of well-being, mood included. There is a connection between the gut and the brain, earning the gut the name of "second brain." Eating a healthy diet that includes probiotics and prebiotics can help promote good gut health, which can have a positive impact on your mood.

Nutrient deficiencies: Nutrient deficiencies, such as low levels of vitamin D or omega-3 fatty acids, have been linked to depression and other mood disorders. Consuming a diet that is rich in nutrients can help support your mental health.

One change in my eating habits inspired by this chapter that might benefit me is: _____

> 4 <
Mental Well-being:

"Being able to be your true self is one of the strongest components of good mental health." -Lauren Fogel Mersy, PsyD. LP

 Mental health is a state of mental well-being that allows people to cope with life's stresses, realize their abilities, learn and work effectively, and contribute to their community. It is an essential component of health and well-being that underpins our individual and collective abilities to make decisions, form relationships, and shape the world in which we live.

Our emotional, psychological, and social well-being contribute to our mental health. It has an impact on how we think, feel, and act. It also influences how we deal with stress, interact with others, and make healthy decisions. Mental health is essential throughout life. However, it is often an area of weakness for people, particularly when lives are in transition.

Mental health is a personal journey that is about developing the security that comes from knowing who we are and where we belong. That is why building relationships that nurture us and provide us with opportunities to develop our unique talents and skills while having meaningful connections to community life is important.

When we do not have a sense of belonging or a stable emotional environment, we can become overwhelmed by the pace of change in our lives. We may feel disconnected from others.

The American gold standard for mental health is equilibrium or balance. Emotional equilibrium, or balance, means that we feel comfortable and secure in our skin and relationships with others. The quality of life that emerges from mental equilibrium and mental health are known.

There are many ways to achieve emotional balance. Feeling secure and well-connected to others, regardless of circumstances, gives a person a stable sense of self-worth and a positive outlook on themselves and their world. This kind of security allows us to keep trying new things and adapting to change more easily.

A healthy lifestyle means doing things that you like, so there is no reason why you can't enjoy life to the fullest. The aim for all aspects of your life is to do what you love, what you find energizing, and what is enjoyable so that it sustains you long-term.

Your mind affects your body, so pay attention to how it's feeling. In addition, recognize negative behavior patterns and learn how to change them. It's easier to change when you feel positive about yourself, so practice positive self-talk daily.

De-stress, Increase positivity:

Positive thinking helps with stress management and can even improve your health. Research finds that positive thinking can be visualized as a mental workout, where you visualize the good things in your life. When you practice positive thinking regularly, the brain processes information better. It can help manage stress, anxiety, and other feelings of negativity by focusing on the good things in life.

When you feel angry or upset, recognize it for what it is (an emotion). Ask yourself this question: "What do I need? What do I want?" Then make a plan as to how you can get what you want.

Calm an anxious mind:

Anxiety is a normal human emotion. However, excessive anxiety levels can result in mental health problems, such as depression and phobias. Over time, anxiety can cause serious social and psychological problems. If you always feel anxious, you may need professional help to manage your symptoms. Although there is no cure for anxiety disorders, effective treatments are available to help you manage your anxiety.

Some tips for calming an anxious mind and de-stressing are:

1) **Mindful breathing** is an effective technique for quickly reducing anger and anxiety. When anxious or angry, you tend to take quick, shallow breaths. This sends a message to your brain, causing a positive feedback loop reinforcing your fight-or-flight response. That's why taking long, deep calming breaths disrupts that loop and helps you calm down.

One breathing technique is three-part breathing. Three-part breathing requires you to take one deep breath in, breathing into your belly, ribcage, and upper chest. Then exhale fully while paying attention to your body.

Once you get comfortable with deep breathing, you can change the ratio of inhalation and exhalation to 1:2 (you slow down your exhalation so that it's twice as long as your inhalation). We all know the calming effect of a long deep breath that allows our lungs to fill with oxygen. This is called diaphragmatic breathing and can be done almost anywhere, anytime. Let your abdomen expand, which allows your lungs to take a deeper breath. Breathe in through the nose for roughly five seconds, then exhale slowly through the mouth for about five seconds.

Do this three or four times, and you'll feel almost immediate stress relief. Some of us spend too much time worrying about what may happen.

2) Visualize yourself at ease.

Use the breathing techniques you've learned in practice. Close your eyes and visualize yourself as calm after taking a few deep breaths. Imagine yourself navigating a stressful or anxiety-inducing situation by remaining calm and focused.

3) Change your focus.

Leave the situation, look in another direction, walk out of the room, or go outside.

Do this exercise so you have time for better decision-making. "We don't do our best thinking when anxious or angry; we engage in survival thinking, but if the situation isn't life-threatening, we want our best thinking, not survival instincts."

4) Relax your shoulders.

If your body is tense, your posture will show it. So, sit tall, take a deep breath, and let your shoulders fall. You can do this by focusing on bringing your shoulder blades together and then down. This lowers your shoulders. Take several deep breaths.

5) Take a break.

Take a break from the situation in which you feel anxious or angry. Tell yourself you will think about it later and put it aside. You'll be less likely to react emotionally with your "fight-or-flight" response, which can make you appear aggressive or intimidating if your body is tense.

6) **Squeeze a stress ball**.

Studies show that, like rubber band balls in the hands, squeeze a stress ball for about four seconds, and your anxiety symptoms decrease by about 80 percent for about 20 minutes. Experts say that squeezing a stress ball releases endorphins, creates positive reinforcement, and makes you feeelmore secure.

7) **Take a brisk walk.**

This relieves tension; you'll feel better if you can shed the stress. Combine it with breathing techniques. A brisk walk can distract your mind and chase away the blues.

8) **Practice yoga.**

Yoga can improve your mood and overall well-being. Yoga may also help you manage your symptoms of depression and anxiety.

10-minute yoga practice for the complete beginner
https://yogawithadriene.com/10-minute-yoga-for-beginners/

20-minute beginner yoga
https://www.youtube.com/watch?v=v7AYKMP6rOE

This simple routine is the perfect way to get going in the morning. Stretch routine in bed.
https://www.youtube.com/watch?v=7iBm75B7LeI&t=19s

Restorative yoga stretches
https://bodybyyoga.training/yoga-for-weight-loss/restorative-yoga-stretches/

There are many yoga videos to watch on YouTube.

9) **Meditate.**

Meditation is a simple practice available to all, which can reduce stress, increase calmness and clarity and promote happiness. Learning how to meditate is straightforward, and the benefits can come quickly. Here, we offer basic tips to get you started on a path toward greater equanimity, acceptance, and joy. Take a deep breath and get ready to relax.

Meditation has been practiced for thousands of years to cultivate awareness of the present moment. This may involve practices to improve focus and attention, connect to the body and breath, accept challenging emotions, and even change consciousness. It has been demonstrated to have a variety of medical and psychological advantages, including stress reduction and enhanced immunity.

Meditation can help you calm your mind. During meditation, you don't react to your thoughts; instead, you observe them. To begin, get into a comfortable seated position and close your eyes. Take a few deep breaths, then resume your regular, even breathing pattern. Focus on your breath as it comes in and out, and return to that focus if your mind wanders. Even a minute of meditation can make a difference.

How to meditate.

- Take a seat. Find a place to sit that feels calm and quiet to you.
- Set a time limit.
- Notice your body.
- Feel your breath.
- Notice when your mind has wandered. Bring it back to focus on your breath.
- Close with kindness.

10) **Caring for a pet** (outward focus); also, stroking a pet is said to be stress-reducing.

11) **Tending plants** and caring for them can lower stress, lower blood pressure, fatigue, and anxiety. Some easy plants to grow: snake plants, spider plants, aloe vera, lavender, basil, lemon balm, and spearmint.

12) **Foods that may reduce stress**. Research suggests that saffron may be effective in treating depression and anxiety.

13) **Listening to the music** of your favorite genre, group, or decade can be soothing.

14) **Whistle or sing an upbeat tune or song**. "Whistle While You Work"

15) **Anticipate a special plan**. Have something to look forward to a hike with a friend; a trip, even local, such as to a museum, a basketball game, or a hockey game; check your town's calendar of events; schedule a one-day class on some topic of interest; volunteer at a fundraising event.

16) **Plan an event**.

Easy event: "Tea with a Topic" – Invite friends. Provide tea and cookies, tea cakes, etc. Some suggestions for topics: bring an item from a collection to share & explain; bring a favorite poem to share, have a speaker. Examples: 1) a story-teller, 2) a representative of a Native American tribe, 3) a speaker from a different culture to explain a celebration in that culture]

17) **A positive, optimistic attitude** lowers blood pressure. It increases happiness, focus & calmness. And putting on a smile de-ages your face!

18) **Friendships** can have an important beneficial effect on your health and well-being. More about this in Chapter 6

Silence your inner critic.

- Try saying, "May I learn to be kinder to myself." Eradicate the negative automatic thoughts that may, unbidden, pop up.

- How? – self-talk If you are sad, nervous, angry, or feel like a failure: "I am sad, but soon I will feel better."

- Feeling a failure: "I have succeeded in many things."

- Have guilt?: "I can learn from my mistakes."

Question your negative feeling

If you are blaming another, look at how you may have contributed.

Letter to self. Write a letter to yourself expressing positivity and compassion. You may have been judgmental about yourself, but in this letter, put that aside and say nice things about yourself.

Tune into your senses. -Name three things you see, smell, taste, feel, or hear.

Friends – It matters with whom you spend time. Connect with friends who uplift you, make you laugh, and make you like yourself when you're with them.

Gratitude – Your positivity can be elevated by focusing attention on those things in your life for which you are grateful.

Mindfulness Strategies to Help You Recharge

A mindfulness technique – The raisin exercise Pick up a raisin and...focus on:

- The way the raisin looks;
- How it feels;
- How the skin responds to its manipulation;

- Its smell;
- Its taste.

By concentrating your attention on the raisin, you won't be focusing on negative energy.

Anxiety and depression

This new freedom retirement brings may not always be glorious and satisfying. If you are experiencing depression, loss of self-esteem, anxiety, feeling worthless, or considering suicide, get help. The following organizations offer help with suicidal thoughts:

- If you're in the United States, you can call or text 988. By calling or texting 988, you'll connect with mental health professionals at the 988 Suicide and Crisis Lifeline, formerly known as the National Suicide Prevention Lifeline
- Also in the U.S., call SAMHSA's National Helpline, 1-800-662-HELP (4357) (also known as the Treatment Referral Routing Service) is a confidential, free, 24-hour-a-day, 365-day-a-year, information service, in English and Spanish, for individuals and family members facing mental and/or substance use disorders. This service provides referrals to local treatment facilities, support groups, and community-based organizations.
- MHAnational.org/crisisresources
- help.org
- psychologytoday.com

Relaxing videos

Beautiful Music www.youtube.com/watch?v=_kT38XB1YHo
Piano Music & Soft Rain Sound
www.youtube.com/watch?v=Lp6XlsBm_Lw
3 Hour Relaxing Guitar Music: Guitar Music: Meditation
Music www.youtube.com/watch?v=ss7EJ-PW2Uk

Combatting loneliness –

Loneliness is a state of mind that we are all familiar with, even if we are hesitant to discuss it. When you notice a gap between your current situation and your desired social life, you may experience a sense of emptiness and longing, which can be associated with various negative emotions. You may feel lonely and bitter if you discover that your friends are socializing without you. You may pine for people who are no longer present, lament past social blunders, or feel disconnected, isolated, or even ashamed that you have difficulty connecting with others and forming new friendships.

Physical isolation, for example, can contribute to loneliness if you isolate yourself from family and friends. Loneliness isn't always about being physically close to other people. However, you can be at a party with a large crowd and still feel lonely. On the other hand, many people live alone and still feel a strong connection to others.

People can be lonely, whether single, married, or have children. Loneliness is one of the main causes of depression and anxiety. When you suffer from loneliness, here are some ways to combat the negative feelings:

Practice self-kindness. In difficult moments, learn to practice self-kindness. Blaming yourself when you feel lonely is not helpful. Limit your hurtful self-talk, and just give yourself a break. Perhaps a walk in nature or a day at the spa may be helpful for getting yourself into a self-kindness mood.

www.psychologytoday.com/us/basics/self-talk

Share a good feeling. When you feel good about something, share it with others right away. Capitalize on the present moment. You could share by calling or texting a friend or family member. The positive things that you can share do not have to be big. Even if it is nothing more than you woke up on the right side of the bed and thought, "Hey, I'm feeling great today!" You can share these moments. Creating small moments of savoring and connection with others can help you overcome loneliness.

www.psychologytoday.com/us/basics/loneliness

Rethink how you spend your spare time. When you feel lonely, sometimes you just want to retreat into a corner and hide. At other times, your endless little tasks leave you too exhausted to go out and be social. But you can get stuck in loneliness by opting to stay alone *every night* with your phone, watching Netflix or Hulu or whatever is on TV, or watching silly videos on YouTube. You are depriving yourself of meaningful social connection, and the only way to get out of it is to start living differently.

Let your loneliness motivate you to reach out to people and strengthen your relationships. By seeking out social support, you can create more social moments with the people in your life who matter to you, and it usually reduces your loneliness.

www.psychologytoday.com/us/blog/click-here-happiness/201803/4-ways-cultivate-kindness-online

Connect in real life. Connecting in real life may not be as easy as it once was. We often default to using our smartphones—it's easier and now culturally accepted.

www.psychologytoday.com/us/blog/click-here-happiness/201806/are-you-phone-addict

But building stronger in-person connections can decrease loneliness. Look people in the eyes, listen, be mindful, and choose not to be distracted by your phone.

https://www.psychologytoday.com/us/basics/mindfulness

Reach out to others. Reach out to a friend, a relative, a neighbor, or even more if that feels more comfortable. Reach out and say hello when you see someone who looks like they need company. Talk to strangers. Research suggests that even seemingly trivial interactions with strangers—like chatting with a cashier or the postman—may reduce feelings of loneliness by helping us feel more socially connected. So, say "hello", ask them how they are, or chat about anything. A small act can make a big difference in keeping loneliness at bay. So, reach out to other human beings. It not only may help you, it may help the other person as well!

Go out with your friends. Socializing with friends can be an excellent way to experience positive emotions again. You can do this by taking your friends on an outing they all enjoyed in the past or planning something new like a family picnic, or going on a date night together.

Face-to-face social interactions tend to improve our mood and reduce depression. Activities that involve other people, such as attending religious services or engaging in sports. are also likely to have positive effects on our mental health —Find ways to be around people more.

https://www.psychologytoday.com/us/basics/depression

Join a hobby group or club.

Plenty of groups are available in your local area, including sports groups, book clubs, dog lovers, and others. Find a fun and interesting group with a common focus, such as photography, juggling, cooking, scuba diving, etc.

Join an organization that provides social activities.

Many local organizations offer a variety of events and activities, including book clubs, trips, music concerts, and bowling. The more you participate in these events, the more opportunities you will have to make new friends.

Be active online.

Instead of passively surfing the net or your social media, if you want to go online, opt instead to do something that involves the active participation of other people. For example, you could play games with others, chat about something you care about, give advice on a forum, or have a video call with a friend. The more you interact with others while online, the more connected you are likely to feel.

Stop your negative thought cycles. We might repeatedly think about what we could have done differently to prevent ourselves from feeling so alone. Ruminating over and over again about the events or people, or causes will not help us solve it. Instead, do something different that stops these thoughts and changes your experience of the world. For example, if you're feeling lonely, go to the gym or schedule lunches with friends. You'll see how that helps!

Share for real online. Instead of posting about things you did, reclaim the word "share" for what it really means—to give a small or large portion of what is yours to someone else. You could share advice, words of support, or even empathy, all from your smartphone. As a result, your connections are likely to be more kind and supportive.

Stop focusing so much on yourself. Instead of focusing on what you can get, focus on what you can give. You could sell T-shirts or craft items online to raise money for a good cause. You could ask friends to donate to a charity for your birthday. By giving to others, you do good and, at the same time, are less lonely.

Generate a sense of awe. Awe (like when we witness the birth of a new baby or a majestic mountain) makes time seem like it's standing still. It helps us be more open to connecting because something about feeling small in the context of a big world appears to help us see ourselves as part of a whole and may help us feel less alone. So, expose yourself to something that creates awe—like landscapes or new experiences.

Spend money on experiences. Instead of spending all your cash on things, spend money on experiences with others. This is way better for our mental health. Get creative and think about what you want to do with others. For example, go wine tasting, go on a canoeing trip, plan a beach party, or host an arts & crafts night. What group activities might make you feel less lonely?

Pay attention to the things that matter. Start paying attention to the present moment. What are the experiences that make you feel lonely? What experiences make you feel connected or like you belong? Limit your engagement in activities that make you feel lonely and partake more in activities that make you feel connected.

Create a vision board. Make much of it about connecting—building community, networking, spending time with family, and the like. Once you discover the things that make you feel less lonely and more connected, plan for what you'll do. Let the vision board be a reminder of what you need to do to combat loneliness.

Tend to your network. Sometimes we can end up feeling alone even though we are connected to lots of people. It can be helpful to reach out to these people and schedule times to catch up. Aim to schedule at least one social hour per week—a coffee date, lunch, or happy hour. Perhaps even an old friendship can be reignited.

Join an online group of like-minded people. You can now find people online with just about any interest —cooking, sports, politics, etc. Joining one of these groups with a theme can be a way to feel more connected to others, even without face-to-face interactions. You might get to know some new people or make lifelong friends. Try out a few groups to see which ones fit you best and decrease loneliness the most.

Volunteer remotely or in real life in your town. You may even find people for good new friend connections. Be sure you're working with others. Working on an important problem with others can help you decrease loneliness, in addition to helping your community.

Be nice to yourself. Practice compassion toward yourself when you fail at something. Everyone fails, and there is no need to feel guilty, bully yourself, or put yourself down. That won't help you decrease loneliness. Instead, try talking to yourself in a supportive, kind, and caring way and resolve to do better next time.

Mental boosts and distractions from current challenges

1. **Enjoy Nature** Spending time in serene natural environments is proven to lower stress levels, improve working memory and provide a sense of rejuvenation.[1]

2. **Perform Random Acts of Kindness**. Be a positive force for others. Doing good for others makes you feel good. It lifts your mood and improves self-esteem and self-worth.

3. **Develop an Attitude of Gratitude.** -A great way to lift your spirits is to notice and appreciate the positives in our lives. Practice being thankful for the simple things in life.

4. **Take a mental break.** Positivity can be killed by exhaustion. When things get overwhelming, take a break, whatever it may be, even a nap.

5. **Laugh.** You've heard that laughter truly is the best medicine for what ails you. It boosts mood, strengthens your immune system, diminishes pain, and protects you from stress.

Watch a comedy on TV. Call or spend some time with a crazy friend who always knows how to make you laugh. Host a game night with your friends.

6. Hang Around with Positive People.

Stress is contagious, but so is happiness.

7. Look for the silver lining in a tough situation

Is there a bright spot? Find it and ease your burden a little. Training your mind this way can transform your whole thought process.

8. Remind yourself not to dwell on negativity

Avoid spending time on downers. Besides bringing you down, it also makes you less effective in tackling other tasks. Negativity breeds negativity. Don't replay bad or unpleasant situations. Bad things happen; have a positive idea ready to replace it.

9. Engage in positive self-talk

A friend of mine liked saying, "It will be all right in the end; if it isn't all right yet, it isn't the end!". You have permission to borrow this!

10. Talk it out with a friend

Talking out a problem with a friend or group of friends helps you hear and understand the problem better. Explain the situation and your feelings. Brainstorming with friends can help you generate new ideas to help you resolve the issue. Emotional support also makes a difference. ...therapy that doesn't cost much!

11. **Channel your anxious energy into something productive.** Clean a room in your house, wash your car, wash your dog, organize a drawer, or do some gardening.

12. **Engage in rigorous exercise.** Exercise has been shown to help reduce anxiety and elevates mood. The "feel good" brain chemicals (neurotransmitters, endorphins, and endocannabinoids) are released, chasing away negativity.

13. **Sleep.** Maintaining a positive attitude supported by proper rest is a critical part of mental health. Don't shortchange yourself on this important effect on your mental state.

14. **Journal.** Journaling is a healthy outlet to express yourself, to deal with overwhelming emotions. Your mental health can be greatly aided by writing down your thoughts, emotions, and ideas. You can even develop a plan to mitigate difficult issues.

15. **Play Hooky.** Think up some total change of pace and take a day or part of a day to paint a picture, kayak down a river, take a one-night camping trip, or watch a "guilty pleasure" movie or program on TV--something fun ...whatever it may be.

16. **Treat yourself**. An effective way to support a positive outlook is to reward yourself with "me time" Celebrate YOU ... who you are as a person. Indulge yourself.

17. **Move through your day mindfully.** Living mindfully means consciously deciding to be fully present at each moment of the day.

Focus on the now, leaving no space for negative thoughts or worry.

18. **Take care of yourself spiritually**

Remember to feed your soul and keep the mind-body-spirit connection strong by engaging in spirit-enhancing, contemplative activities such as meditation, prayer, reading spiritual materials, and/or attending religious services.

19. **Celebrate small wins**

Celebrate the things you got right today and the things you do well. Have success in improving a habit? Celebrate! Did you add two more burpee repetitions today? Yay! Celebrate! Haven't reached your final goal but have made progress along the way? Yes!! Celebrate! It's a myth that you can only claim success once you've reached that end goal.

20. **Savoring**:

Think back to a wonderful trip, experience, or time spent with a friend or even on your own.

21 **Watch birds** "Watching birds is relaxing and can be a stress reliever." Emma Greig, Cornell Lab of Ornithology

22. **Chocolate**

One of the world's favorite foods and is #1 on people's craving list. With over 1,500 chemical compounds, chocolate is one of the most chemically complex foods of all. Why do you feel wonderful when you indulge in chocolate? It's a great source of tryptophan, the amino acid precursor of serotonin as well as a source of magnesium, an anti-stress mineral.

www.sciencedaily.com/releases/2007/09/070911073921.htm
www.science.org.au/curious/everything-else/chocolate

Chocolate is one of few dietary sources of *anandamide*, a naturally occurring neurotransmitter referred to as the "bliss molecule.", providing happiness and mental balance.
https://pubmed.ncbi.nlm.nih.gov/11363932/

Good news as we age: Chocolate can help seniors with short-term memory loss and prevent mental decline.

www.sciencedaily.com/releases/2007/02/070221101326.htm
Lower your risk of dementia by eating your dose of chocolate! Flavonoids are powerful antioxidant substances contained in chocolate and are also found in wine, tea, fruits, and vegetables The flavonoids have been thought to offer protection associated with a lower incidence of dementia in a cohort of 1367 subjects above 65 years of age.

Recommended daily serving: one ounce of dark chocolate daily, per the Cleveland Clinic. https://bebrainfit.com/brain-foods

"All you need is love. But a little chocolate now and then doesn't hurt."

  — Charles M. Schulz

A Mindfulness Strategy to Help You Recharge

The Body Scan

Step 1: The Body Scan begins with lying on your back with your palms facing up and your feet falling slightly apart. This exercise can also be done sitting on a comfortable chair with feet resting on the floor;

Step 2: Lie very still for the duration of the exercise, and move with awareness if it becomes necessary to adjust your position.

Step 3: Next, begin by bringing awareness to the breath, noticing the rhythm, the experience of breathing in and expelling out. You should not try to change the way you are breathing but rather just be gently aware of your breath.

Step 4: Now direct your attention to the body: how it feels, the texture of clothing against the skin, the contours of the surface on which the body is resting, the temperature of the body and the environment.

Step 5: Then guide your awareness to the parts of the body that are tingling, sore, or feeling, particularly heavy or light; note any areas of your body where you don't feel any sensations at all or are hypersensitive.

Next, run your attention through each part of the body, paying special attention to the way each area feels. Start at the feet and move upwards as follows:

- Toes of both feet
- The rest of the feet (top, bottom, ankle)
- Lower legs
- Knees
- Thighs
- Pelvic region (buttocks, tailbone, pelvic bone, genitals)
- Abdomen
- Chest

- Lower back
- Upper back (back ribs & shoulder blades)
- Hands (fingers, palms, backs, wrists)
- Arms (lower, elbows, upper)
- Neck
- Face and head (jaw, mouth, nose, cheeks, ears, eyes, forehead, scalp, back & top of the head)

Happiness Boost: Develop your sense of wonder and awe

A distressed mind can be soothed by cultivating a sense of wonder and awe. Consider these; develop your own list.

- Vastness – Grand Canon, starry heavens
- Synergy
- How is it possible? – airplanes, bridge buildings spanning wide rivers, spiders connecting a thread across a wide distance
- Beautifully crafted music
- Inexplicable coincidences
- People's courage -that's moral beauty
- Bravery, e.g, Schindler's list
- Machines
- Buildings
- Painting (How about the Sistine Chapel?)
- Jewels, e.g., Hiddenite emerald
- Helenite: emerald obsidianite from the fused volcanic rock dust from Mount St. Helens
  https://geologylearn.blogspot.com/2016/12/hiddenite.html
- One's own body - healing a cut, feeding its growth, and repairing needs from the food we eat.
- A dog's ability to follow a trail or detect C-diff disease or cancer, or warn of an impending epileptic episode
- Three-year-old child playing skillfully on a violin
- Scientific discoveries
- Something larger than oneself, to get beyond oneself.

<u>What would you add to this list?</u>

Indulge in some carefree joy; release happy hormones:

- Hot air balloon ride
- Go to Pike's Fish Market (Seattle)
- Watch funny dog, cat, or other animal videos
- Smile. It can boost your mood and make others smile back.
- Write a thank-you note to yourself or someone else. It can help you appreciate what you have and express gratitude.
- Go for a walk, a bike ride, or a picnic.
- Indulge in a delicious piece of chocolate or a fresh, colorful smoothie.
- Find a piece of jewelry you haven't worn in a while. It can make you feel like you have something new and special.
- Talk to a stranger. It can spark a connection and a positive interaction.
- Send snail mail to a friend. It can surprise them and make them feel loved.
- Watch the sunrise. It can inspire you with its beauty and remind you of the possibilities of a new day.
- Do a project you've meant to do; there's joy in accomplishing it.
- Create a celebration for something, anything.

These are just some examples of things that can bring you joy. You can also try other activities that suit your personality and passions. The important thing is to find what makes you happy and do it often.

Sleep

Your mental well-being can be affected by your quality of sleep.

A proper night's sleep is important. A good night's sleep can be affected by a wide range of influences. However, getting good sleep can be difficult at times.

It's possible that you have no control over the things that keep you from sleeping. You may, however, develop routines that promote healthier sleeping.

Tips to aid sleep:

1. Stick to a sleep schedule

Set aside no more than eight hours for sleep. The recommended amount of sleep for a healthy adult is at least seven hours. Most people don't need more than eight hours in bed to be well rested.

Go to bed and get up at the same time every day, including weekends. Being consistent reinforces your body's sleep-wake cycle.

If you don't fall asleep within about 20 minutes of going to bed, leave your bedroom and do something relaxing. Read or listen to soothing music. Go back to bed when you're tired. Repeat as needed but continue to maintain your sleep schedule and wake-up time. It is recommended that you not watch TV or do something on your phone because the screen can emit blue light that has been found to disrupt the sleep cycle [from the Sleep Foundation]

2. Pay attention to what you eat and drink

Don't go to bed hungry or stuffed. Avoid heavy or large meals within a couple of hours of bedtime. Discomfort might keep you up.

Nicotine, caffeine, and alcohol deserve caution, too. The stimulating effects of nicotine and caffeine take hours to wear off and can interfere with sleep. And even though alcohol might make you feel sleepy at first, it can disrupt sleep later in the night.

3. Create a restful environment

Keep your room cool, dark, and quiet. Exposure to light in the evenings might make it more challenging to fall asleep. Consider using room-darkening shades, earplugs, a fan, or other devices to create an environment that suits your needs. Even during sleep, your body can recognize when there's too much light in your bedroom. Your heart rate increases and your quality of sleep suffers.

A metronome light can promote deep, peaceful sleep. It is scientifically designed to block out overactive thought patterns. It essentially combines yoga, meditation, and behavioral therapy! This makes it the safe way to effortlessly fall asleep.

www.menshealth.com/technology-gear/g23397130/best-sleep-tech/

4. Doing calming activities before bedtime, such as taking a bath or using relaxation techniques, might promote better sleep.

5. Limit daytime naps

Long daytime naps can interfere with nighttime sleep. Limit naps to no more than one hour and avoid napping late in the day.

6. Include physical activity in your daily routine.

Regular physical activity can promote better sleep, but not too close to bedtime.

Spending time outside every day might be helpful, too.

7. Manage worries

Try to resolve your worries or concerns before bedtime. Jot down what's on your mind and then set it aside for tomorrow.

Stress management might help. Start with the basics, such as getting organized, setting priorities, and delegating tasks. Meditation also can ease anxiety.

8. Aromatherapy:

Essential oils such as lavender, peppermint, and cedarwood are helpful in promoting sleep. Use an oil diffuser before you fall asleep, or put a touch on your pillow or bed sheet.

Ylang-ylang has been found in research to boost mood, reduce depression, alleviate anxiety, lower blood pressure, decrease heart rate, stimulate oil production in the skin and on the scalp, and last (but maybe not least), repel flying insects and kill bug larvae.

https://www.youngliving.com/blog/oils-for-sleep

Saying "no"

You may have more time now and think you can do it all. Don't take on too much as you plan your time. You may have to exercise your prerogative to say "No."

Take a walk down memory lane with music of the 50's, 60's, 70's: Seek some tunes on the internet https://renewmusic.com/channels .

An idea from this chapter that can help me increase my positive outlook is: _____

_____

> 5 <
Enriching Your Brain:

"If the human brain were so simple that we could understand it, we would be so simple that we couldn't."

– Emerson M. Pugh

 Brain exercises are one of the ways to keep your brain young.

Exercises for Brain Fitness:

Crossword puzzles:

Crossword puzzles are a classic way to challenge and engage the brain. They require problem-solving, vocabulary skills, and pattern recognition to complete. By solving crossword puzzles regularly, you can improve your memory, focus, and cognitive abilities. You can find crossword puzzles in newspapers, magazines, or through various online resources.

Sudoku

Sudoku is a number-based puzzle game that requires logical thinking and problem-solving skills. Regularly playing Sudoku can help improve memory, concentration, and overall cognitive function.

Jigsaw puzzles:

Jigsaw puzzles are another excellent way to exercise your brain. They require spatial awareness, pattern recognition, and problem-solving skills to complete. Assembling jigsaw puzzles stimulates both the left and right hemispheres of the brain, promoting mental dexterity and cognitive function. They come in various sizes, difficulty levels, and themes, both in physical and digital formats.

Card games:

Card games, such as bridge, poker, and solitaire, can provide mental stimulation and challenge cognitive skills, including memory, strategy, and pattern recognition. Playing with others can also foster social interaction and improve communication skills.

Brain Gym exercises:

Brain Gym exercises are designed to improve cognitive function, enhance learning, and support a healthy brain. Some specific exercises include:

Cross Crawl:

This exercise involves touching the opposite knee or elbow while marching in place. It helps to improve coordination, balance, and focus, as it engages both the left and right hemispheres of the brain.

Lazy Eights:

In this exercise, you draw figure eight (or infinity symbol) in the air with your index finger, alternating hands. Lazy Eights can improve hand-eye coordination, visual tracking, and fine motor skills.

Assorted Word Games online

The well-known dictionary website provides many games and quizzes to keep you mentally sharp:

www.merriam-webster.com/games

Other Ways to Stimulate your brain

Try these eight ways of enriching your brain in a more balanced way:

1. Practice the art of conversation: Talking with people who are different from us helps us stretch our brains and make new connections among wide-ranging topics.

2. Learn something new every day. Learning a new skill or vocabulary literally makes the relevant brain areas larger and better connected.

3. Take up a musical instrument. To get the most benefit, try keyboard instruments like the piano or organ because they stimulate both sides of the brain equally. The more proficient you become with an instrument, the more your brain will adapt to recruiting more motor regions on either side of the brain, known as neuroplasticity.

4. Experiment with art: If you have a passion for art, it will enrich your life and make your brain healthier. You can see examples here: www.healing-power-of-art.org/art-and-the-brain

5. Join a club: keep your brain active as you age by joining activities like sports, reading groups, writing groups, etc. The more active you are, the healthier your brain will stay longer.

6. Stay focused and clear: Take time to analyze what you have done so that you can understand where you are going and also focus on your work. The more we think about the past, the more our brain stores those memories.

7. Be a spectator: Sometimes, when we have done our work in a particular field, we tend to think that we know everything about it; however, in reality, there is always something new that one can learn by being a "spectator." It helps one's mind to open up to different possibilities of expression and process.

8. Use music: Music is a great way to keep your brain healthy because it helps you relax, be calm and follow a particular rhythm. With this, you can improve your concentration and focus, which are very important. Developing skills in learning music also helps to develop memory and improve brain functions in all areas of life.

Have fun: You can try any of the above activities, but if you aren't enjoying it, it will not be beneficial. It is essential to have fun with the things that you are doing.

Note: These activities are for people who are interested in enhancing their creative abilities. Thus, "artistic" and "creative" have been used frequently. If there are no such interests, try new hobbies involving physical activities like cooking food or gardening.

Increase vocabulary:

By increasing your vocabulary, you can increase your understanding of things around you, thus keeping your mind young. You'll have an increased ability to read fluently with good accuracy and understanding. An increase in reading ability increases your overall brain power.

Read aloud: This improves our ability to parse spoken language and improve verbal memory, thereby increasing our mental processing speed.

Increase verbal memory – vocabulary: This is the general term for remembering things we hear or see (verbal memory). It is part of our memory system that allows us to relate an auditory item to a visual one or a written item to its spoken counterpart.

The memory may slow down; that's a common experience. There are ways you can aid memory.

For example, if you're trying to remember names: when you're meeting someone, and they tell you their name, use the person's name in the conversation (don't overdo it)

- Ask questions about their name—Origin? Spelling? Meaning?
- Create visual image to associate: Andrew – "He reached in and drew a winning number"; Beth – picture queen Elizabeth I; Mabel – make a table.
- End the conversation with their name.

Learn a New Language

Some of the benefits: It stimulates your brain, improves attention span and memory, builds multitasking skills, boosts your creativity, slows down cognitive decline, and improves your first language!

https://potomac.edu/benefits-of-learning-a-second-language/

Reading, Writing, and more

Reading improves your memory in retaining information, and improves eye-hand coordination.

Moreover, it forces you to participate intellectually and improves the way you think about situations which can benefit learning in many other ways.

Read aloud to someone.

Write letters to friends at a distance.

Engage in other activities, such as talking with others, listening to exciting stories, or watching a good movie.

Stimulate your brain with movement:

Go for a walk or ride your bike instead of driving. It does not have to be extended; 10-15 minutes is enough to stimulate your brain and make it work better.

Try hand-eye coordination – if you have had issues involving sports or any other activities, then try these activities which can help increase your focus, accuracy, and processing speed: jumping rope, jumping jacks, and other physical exercises like yoga or meditation. They also provide a form of relaxation in addition to improving focus and concentration.

Use Humor:

Humor is an excellent way of keeping your brain young and active. When you laugh, your brain releases chemicals such as endorphins, dopamine, and serotonin that help to keep you happy.

You can use humor in many ways to improve your memory recall and reduce stress levels which have been linked to some forms of depression. Humor is used in therapy as a way of helping people remember information more quickly.

Always try to find humor in everything because it can help distract you from meaningless tasks and help make life a little more enjoyable.

An anecdote is a short amusing, or interesting story about a real incident or a person; for example, one of a teacher friend's third graders was wearing a Fitbit watch, which prompted the teacher to ask, "Are you tracking your steps?" "No," said the little girl. "I wear this for Mommy so she can show Daddy when he gets home."

Be active:

Aspects of your daily life can be a good way of keeping your brain young and active, such as playing sports, going out for walks, or running around aimlessly. Being active can increase mental energy and mental stamina as well as help avoid diseases such as depression which inhibit brain power. If you are not a physically active person and feel that you would like to be, then think about how you can modify your daily life to do things in a more physically active way.

Researchers have found that doing just 15 minutes of aerobic exercise three times a week can substantially reduce your risk for Alzheimer's, dementia, and Parkinson's diseases because it will help clear out the amyloid plaques and tau tangles in your brain associated with these diseases. Exercising the brain helps facilitate alpha wave generation, which helps keep your mind young. Alpha waves are required for long-term memory formation and conscious thought.

Change up something:

 You can change your habits, such as how you eat, spend time with others, or even your clothing.

Socialize:

Socializing is when you spend time with others, such as friends, family, or even online friends. Socialization can improve critical thinking skills since it involves the process of thinking through situations and planning in case those situations occur. It also improves your problem-solving ability by thinking creatively rather than relying on only one approach.

Seek joy:

Finding joy within yourself and your surroundings can get you through the day, especially when you are having a difficult day. Joy helps maintain a positive attitude, which is essential for good health and personal relationships.

The things that bring you joy can be simple and small, such as reading a good book, watching a funny movie, or talking with someone who makes you feel good.

Studies have shown that people who find joy in their lives are generally healthier in many ways than those who do not. They also tend to live longer and have better overall life satisfaction.

One way to find joy is by participating in activities that make you feel good. This can involve learning a new skill such as cooking, dancing, or sports.

Setting goals for yourself and working towards them is another way to find joy. You should set goals for your future and what you want your life to look like, which can be a helpful way of boosting the amount of happiness that you have in life.

Be creative:

Creative thinking involves an integrative process of problem-solving, innovation, pattern recognition, and imagination, and it is an essential component of the brain power cycle because it helps your brain store and retrieve information more efficiently. You can keep a journal, challenge your body, meditate, and more.

Food for the brain

For proper brain function and power, certain foods assist in increasing brain power. There are essential foods for brain power, like certain kinds of fish, leafy green vegetables, nuts, and other foods that help protect your brain.

1) Fish: Inadequate Omega-3 fatty acids have been linked to depression and anxiety. Cold water fatty fish like salmon, mackerel, and herring are natural sources of Omega 3 fatty acids.

2) Leafy Green Vegetables: These vegetables, like spinach, lettuce, and kale, contain high levels of magnesium, which boosts the production of neurotransmitters in the brain. Neurotransmitters are chemical messengers that facilitate communication between different nerve cells.

3) Nuts: Omega 3 fatty acids are found in nuts like walnuts, almonds, sunflower seeds, and pine nuts. They may help promote brain and heart health, and reduce inflammation. See more benefits at https://healthline.com/nutrition/17-health-benefits-of-omega-3 However, a National Institute of Health study found that Omega 6 fatty acids (common in processed foods such as cookies and crackers, as well as in fast food and fried foods) have been linked to obesity.

Other foods that you can add to your diet or find in your kitchen are protein- and iron-rich foods like meats, eggs, and other seafood are great sources (tasty food, too!). Also, try getting more fruits, vegetables, and whole grains which contain vitamins that help your brain power. Coffee also has been linked to memory skill development and improvement of cognitive function.

The herb rosemary has beneficial effects on memory and cognition. Resveratrol (in berries, dark chocolate)and red wine offer brain-boosting benefits.

- Kale - may help slow the loss of memory and thinking skills.
- Eggs are rich in vitamin D, which research has found may help protect against memory loss and forgetfulness.
- Avocados have B vitamins that studies have found may boost mood, reduce anxiety and relieve irritability.
- Lemons and limes: A naturally occurring compound in citrus fruits may help safeguard the brain's nerve cells.
- Walnuts – have compounds that assist thinking and reasoning.
- Beans – Vitamin B9 may help guard against memory loss.
- Blueberries improve communication between brain cells.
- Rolled oats and other grains supply glucose to fuel the brain (and fiber to help digestion).
- Extra-virgin olive oil: Compounds found in this oil may increase mental focus and slow a decline in thinking skills, researchers say.
- Coconuts are not only delicious but also packed with nutrients. In particular, coconut is rich in antioxidants, has powerful antibacterial properties, and may support better blood sugar control. [Healthline.com]

https://stayingsharp.aarp.org/themes/superfoods-brain/

This chapter gave me the ideas of adding _____, _____, and _____ to improve my brain's best functioning.

> 6 <
Relationships with others:

"Friendship ... is born when one man says to another, "What! You too? I thought that no one but myself..." — C.S. Lewis, *The Four Loves*

"A friend is someone who knows all about you and still loves you." — Elbert Hubbard

Importance of Friendship

It's important to work not only on our relationship with ourselves but also with others. Friendships enrich your life and improve your health and well-being. However, it is not always easy to develop or maintain friendships.

Benefits of friendships—Friends can:

- help provide support during bad times and help you celebrate good times.
- prevent loneliness and isolation. Companionship can be rewarding.
- increase a sense of purpose, self-worth, and of belonging.
- increase your happiness.
- reduce stress and depression.
- Improve self-confidence.
- help you cope with traumas, such as serious illness, divorce or death of a loved one.
- encourage you to avoid unhealthy lifestyle habits, such as lack of exercise or excessive drinking.
- listen — really listen — to your problems,
- help distract you when you feel sad or upset.
- validate your feelings,
- do nice things for you "just because",
- may help you live longer!

www.mayoclinic.org/healthy-lifestyle/adult-health/in-depth/friendships/art-20044860

Adults with strong social connections have a reduced risk of many significant health problems, including depression, high blood pressure and an unhealthy body mass index (BMI). In fact, studies have found that older adults who have meaningful relationships and social support are likely to live longer than their peers with fewer connections.

- Social relationships are related to longevity. www.pnas.org/doi/abs/10.1073/pnas.1511085112
- Connection improves our overall well-being. Close friendships make us happier. www.researchgate.net/publication/23545596

If you have a romantic relationship, you might go to your partner first. Romantic partners can absolutely offer comfort and reassurance. However, they shouldn't be your only source of emotional support.

You can show your love for your partner in many ways. If you want to be more romantic, try going out into nature (such as on a hike or walking on the beach), making a meal with some fresh ingredients, or showing them how much you care for them by doing something nice for them like taking care of the laundry or cleaning their house. Be yourself, and be open to new suggestions. Take time for your spouse or partner every day.

Sit down and talk at the end of the night. It is so important to maintain your strong relationship, stay involved in each other's lives, and share any problems that either of you is facing. Relationships take continuous work to be successful, so take the time to nourish yours every day in some sort of way.

Our relationships with others must also be mutually respectful, honest, open-minded, and collaborative. It's important to accept everyone has flaws and try to work through them together. This can be not easy, but it is worth it. It's important to make sure you don't just judge others or make decisions based solely on emotions; this can often lead to disappointment, resentment, and being stuck in the past.

Remember that while we are all different, we have commonalities that allow us to relate to one another. It is important to acknowledge these differences and challenges and embrace them as part of what makes each of us a person.

While it's not easy to establish new relationships with others, it can be a very worthwhile investment of your effort. Also, remember that the relationships you have built in your past are still there but will change.

To help maintain these relationships, try to contact a friend or family member each day. This can allow you to develop a support network of people with whom you can talk and share experiences and problems. People who can help you see things from other perspectives, give advice, and offer encouragement. Talking with others about your struggles, difficulties, and sometimes even successes helps provide a baseline of truth and reality against which you can see unacceptable or troubling behaviors.

Everyone's past is different from yours but acknowledging these differences can enrich your mutual relationship. Be open to the advice of others with more experience in certain areas than you have.

People talk and interact with one another for different reasons. Some may want to be close friends; others may want to talk occasionally on the phone. Put judgment aside and accept the individual as they are. Create a relationship-building plan that fits the needs of all parties.

If you have been disappointed by someone in your past, it is important to forgive them now to move forward.

Intergenerational relationships are important since they teach us about compassion and understanding.

Why might it be hard to make friends or maintain friendships?

This may be challenging, especially when dealing with old patterns.

A change in your life may cause you to grow apart from friends. Perhaps you have moved to a new community and haven't yet found a way to meet people.

It takes effort to develop and maintain good friendships. In numbers of friends, quality counts more than quantity. Close, meaningful relationships are the most worthwhile.

Ways to meet and make new friends

- Stay in touch with people with whom you've worked or taken classes.
- Reconnect with old friends.
- Have you enjoyed chatting with someone at social gatherings? Reach out to them!
- Has someone with whom you've interacted made a positive impression on you? Reach out to them!
- Introduce yourself to neighbors.
- Even reach out to family members to get to know someone better...a cousin, maybe?
- Attend community events.
- Volunteer. See Chapter 8

- Extend and accept invitations.
- Take up a new interest.
- Join a faith community.
- Take a walk.

Meetup groups cater to many interests. They are often organized online, so you can search for your particular interest area, then attend an in-person gathering.

You can take an online friendship into an IRL (that's "In Real Life") friend with potentially life-changing benefits. Unlike taking a romantic connection from a dating app to an actual date, how to make a friend relationship is less clear. https://www.meetup.com/blog/how-to-turn-an-online-connection-into-an-irl-friend/

If you're in a Meetup group that usually gathers online, and perhaps you've attended two or three events, you may have found yourself building rapport with the same few people.

You may find you can build stronger connections. You have identified what you have in common because you've met in a Meetup group or at an online event.

Being in a group can stave off loneliness and isolation.

Draw Upon the People You Have.

Recognize that you don't have to keep everyone in your life just because they've been there before. However, some of these people can be useful resources to expand your friend group.

Suppose there's an alumni group in your community. Sign up for events when available. Cast a wide net to find a small group of people who will eventually be great friends.

Figure Out What Matters to You.

Focus on what matters to you, then intentionally put yourself in those places with those people.

For example, if you like hiking, find a group that does that. Sometimes you can form a group of people with a common interest via a social media group such as NextDoor.com.

Push Yourself Outside of Your Comfort Zone.

Say **'yes'** to invitations, to join groups and organizations, and to any opportunity that puts you in a room (literally or figuratively) with others. You'll meet many great people and build some truly meaningful friendships.

Push yourself outside of your comfort zone. Be safe! But remember that no one will stop by that couch in your apartment to make friends with you.

Put in the Work.

All relationships take work ...to start, to maintain. It may be odd to think of them this way, especially regarding friends. But no effective relationship is one-sided, and you must reach out, show up, and demonstrate an interest in other people.

Invest intentionally and wisely in your friendships and reap the rewards.

psychologytoday.com/us/contributors/allison-e-mcwilliams-phd
[Allison McWilliams, Ph.D., is Assistant Vice President of Mentoring and Alumni Personal and Career Development at Wake Forest University.]

Finding new friends and romantic relationships:

Joining a class or community group is a great way to make new friends. If you are shy, start by inviting yourself to someone else's house, and once you feel comfortable, ask them if they would like to go out to coffee or a party with you. Start small and work your way up. Be yourself but be willing to try new things and new ways of doing things.

When you find yourself in a romantic or friend relationship, ensure you take care of the relationship. A healthy relationship will serve as a great support system for your life, and this can help ease stress. Give your relationships the care they need, so they will continue in the future.

If a relationship is not working out, respect the other's feelings. If you are patient, listen to the other, respect their boundaries, and even decide to go your own ways, that's all right.

Building trusting relationships:

Trust is important in a relationship; however, it can be difficult if someone is not open to you. Trust takes time and effort to grow. You can build trust even if you do not know them well. Remember that people like people who are similar to them, so if you show them some of your interests, you may win their trust more quickly. It's important for people to feel comfortable with how they are – that includes how they dress, speak, and their interests. Be dependable and follow through with your actions. Learn how to communicate effectively with others. Remind yourself that it takes time to build and earn trust.

Robert Waldinger, MD, author of The Good Life, appeared on the podcast of The People's Pharmacy (4/22/23) and explained that the key to *eudaimonic* happiness (the longer-term kind of happiness achieved through experiences of meaning and purpose) and finding a way to make life meaningful is connections with other people. This is based on over 80 years of the Harvard Study of Adult Development.

How to nurture your friendships:

- **Be kind.** Exhibit an attitude of gratitude; avoid criticism and negativity.

- **Be a good listener.** Take an interest in your friends' lives. Let the other person know you are paying close attention through eye contact, body language and occasional brief comments such as, "That sounds like fun." When friends share details of hard times or difficult experiences, be empathetic, but don't give advice unless your friends ask for it. That was said to be Thomas Jefferson's standard!

- **Open up.** Build intimacy with your friends by opening up about yourself. Being willing to disclose personal experiences and concerns shows that your friend holds a special place in your life, and it may deepen your connection.

- **Show that you can be trusted.** Being responsible, reliable and dependable is key to forming strong friendships. Keep your engagements and arrive on time. Follow through on commitments you've made to your friends. When your friends share confidential information, keep it private.

- **Make yourself available.** Building a close friendship takes time — together. Make an effort to see new friends regularly, and to check in with them in between meet ups. You may feel awkward the first few times you talk on the phone or get together, but this feeling is likely to pass as you get more comfortable with each other.

- **Manage your nerves with mindfulness.** You may find yourself imagining the worst of social situations, and you may feel tempted to stay home. Use mindfulness exercises to reshape your thinking. Each time you imagine the worst, pay attention to how often the embarrassing situations you're afraid of actually take place. You may notice that the scenarios you fear usually don't happen.

- **Plan special events.** You can host a garden party and invite some people to come. You can also ask your friends out to dinner and make it a night to remember. These special events will help you feel better about yourself and will also help you create more memories for the future. You can also have game nights and trivia nights with others.

  These memories can be shared with your friends and loved ones, which will help you feel closer to them and increase the enjoyment of the event.

- **Make plans with others**. It is important not just to make plans for yourself but to make plans with others and involve your friends in them. It will help you develop a better relationship with those you enjoy spending time with. You can have fun doing activities together, going to dinner, visiting museums and other special places. This is a great way to create memories that you will cherish forever.

- When embarrassing situations do happen, remind yourself that your feelings will pass, and you can handle them until they do.

I   intend   to   connect   with   my   old   friend
_____   and   use   the   plan   of

_____
to find some new friends._

> 7 <
Good Lifestyle Patterns

"Good habits are as addictive as bad habits and a lot more rewarding." — Harvey MacKay

"All of our life is but a mass of small habits - practical, emotional, intellectual and spiritual - that bear us irresistibly toward our destiny." -- William James

 Establishing positive lifestyle patterns is a good way to help balance healthy aging and thriving. Positive, meaningful activities engage your senses, stimulate brain function, and can improve health and well-being. Everyone has their own unique and special pattern that works for them. Some enjoy a busy lifestyle and like to fill their days in an energy-charged way. Some want to take it easy, using more quiet pursuits.

Others like to maintain a balance through a combination of activity, rest, and reflection. Whatever your choice, keep it flexible enough to handle daily life without unnecessary stress or strain. Be a lifelong learner, with or without formal schooling. Keep yourself mentally active by learning new things from new sources. Consider doing crossword puzzles, reading the paper, studying a foreign language, and writing poetry or short stories. If you want to learn more about something that intrigues you, sign up for an adult education class through your local library or community center. Many public libraries now offer classes geared to older adults and their needs. Some community colleges and universities provide evening, weekend, and online courses.

Build Good Habits:

Good habits can inspire you to fulfill your goals and dreams. Good habits are great for building a healthy lifestyle and maintaining a productive living. Bad habits may become barriers to the future you want. To develop positive lifestyle patterns, focus on creating new positive routines and breaking bad routines. You can vow to break a bad habit every time you start one. You can also make a promise vowing that whenever you find yourself starting to do that bad habit of any kind, you will immediately do something in its place that is a better choice.

Wasting time impedes what you want to do with your life. Be intentional.

Habits take 21 days to become a desired pattern in your life, or one you want to get rid of.

Change is key to building positive lifestyle patterns that support healthy aging and thriving. The key to change is to start small, like adding a few more minutes during a workout or sharing more meals with friends. Don't try to change everything at once. Mixing things up so frequently can bring variety into your life and give your brain new experiences. "Small changes make big differences," as the saying goes, especially when learning new things and improving skills.*

Now more than ever, avoid getting stuck in one place or way of doing things.

Good habits to follow or initiate:

1. Adopt an exercise routine and stick to it.

2. Improve your sleep hygiene.

Proper sleep is required for the body to operate properly, and if you are sleep-deprived, you are more likely to have an accident at home. You may also need to change your bedroom, such as hanging room-darkening curtains, to promote better slumber. Make your bed every day! After doing your stretching routine, get up and make the bed. It will set a good tone for the day!

3. Every day, check in with someone. If you have a partner living with you, this is automatic. Do regular daily check-ins with someone so that person will be aware if a health incident happens.

4. Learn to Unwind. Mental wellness is crucial. You should learn relaxation methods like meditation and deep breathing. Identify a few stress-relieving activities and do one or more of them at least once daily.

5. Make Your Home More Secure. One of the simplest lifestyle changes is to perform minor house maintenance to improve the safety of your living environment. Shower handles and a nonskid mat in the tub or shower can assure better safety and help you avoid a significant injury.

6. Find new ways to laugh every day. Laughter is still one of the most effective forms of therapy. Laughing fosters a positive attitude, which can benefit physical and mental well-being. Two ideas: purchase a joke-a-day calendar or watch a comedy program. Finding things to laugh about can even become a pastime that improves the mood.

7. Write in a gratitude journal every night to give yourself a tangible reminder of the good things you have in your life.

8. Take on a difficult task or hobby.

9. Challenges help to strengthen neural links in the brain.

10. Schedule regular check-ups with a doctor.

11. Regular health exams and medical screenings are important, now more than ever. Some people visit their doctors routinely, while others avoid these appointments at all costs.

12. Be sure you have copies of your important papers where you (or someone else, if necessary) can find them.

13. Build in routine activities such as backing up your computer each Friday or paying bills the first and 15th of the month.

14. Consolidate errands.

Break Bad habits:

It's easy to form bad habits but to improve your well-being, increase longevity, and extend your independence., be honest about what you may need to change.

Examples of bad habits that you may need to break are:

1. Not Being Active Enough

A sedentary lifestyle may result in poor bone health and an increased chance of accidents, injuries, and infections. develop a healthy exercise routine, including joining a gym, taking dancing classes, working in the yard, or walking or running in charity marathons.

2. Being Isolated

Withdrawing from family and friends can harm one's physical, mental, and emotional well-being. Seniors who maintain social lives can share their emotions with others rather than having them bottled up inside. Socialization can also encourage physical and mental activity, improving a senior's general well-being.

3. Sleeping Inadequately

Inadequate sleeping patterns are prevalent in the elderly, and the bad habit may lead to low metabolism, heart disease, dementia, or insomnia. Encourage your loved one to have a regular bedtime ritual and to get at least eight hours of sleep each night.

4. Overeating

Excessive eating causes the stomach to expand and the body to create more hydrochloric acid, which can accumulate in the esophagus. Consequently, the likelihood of heartburn rises. Overeating can also cause insulin issues and disrupt blood and oxygen flow to the brain.

5. Poor Stress Management

Poor stress management can increase the likelihood of a stroke or heart attack and increase cognitive loss. On the other hand, learning how to manage anxiety levels can reduce the chance of depression and improve the quality of life. See the stress-management strategies in Chapter 4,

6. Smoking - It's not easy to change this one. There are many methods —cold turkey, nicotine gum, and others. You may find some help online by searching "quit now."

   1-800-QUIT-NOW is the national portal to a network of state quitlines. Quitlines offer evidence-based support, like counseling, referrals to local programs, and free medication—to people who want to quit tobacco.

Another method is Cognitive Behavioral Quitting (CBQ) which helps you stop the thinking and behavioral patterns that keep you addicted to nicotine.

Enlisting a friend to help encourage you and check in with you may help keep you on track to quitting.

7. Drinking - Alcohol consumption can lead to cancer, liver damage, and immune system problems. Wine is just as unhealthy as other alcoholic drinks. Alcohol's effect on the heart (from National Institute of Health)[5] is confusing because some studies have claimed that small amounts of alcohol, particularly red wine, can be beneficial. Past research suggested that alcohol raises HDL, the "good" cholesterol, and that resveratrol, an antioxidant found in grapes (and red wine), has heart-protective properties. However, said Mariann Piano, a professor of nursing at Vanderbilt University, "There's been a lot of recent evidence that has really challenged the notion of any kind of what we call a cardio-protective or healthy effect of alcohol."

www.nytimes.com/2023/01/13/well/mind/alcohol-health-effects.html

And from the Washington Post:

www.washingtonpost.com/wellness/2023/03/31/moderate-drinking-alcohol-wine-risks/

And Bloomberg:

www.bloomberg.com/news/articles/2022-01-20/is-a-glass-of-wine-a-day-good-for-me-heart-federation-says-no

---

[5] www.ncbi.nlm.nih.gov/pmc/articles/PMC5513687/

In conclusion, breaking old habits isn't easy, but you can overcome them with proper motivation and encouragement.

Don't wait any longer to take control of your health and well-being. Start making these positive lifestyle changes today and enjoy the benefits of a healthier, happier, and more fulfilling life.

A good habit I intend to cultivate is

_____

and a bad habit I hope to eliminate is

_____

> 8 <
New Endeavors:

"You are never too old to set another goal or to dream a new dream" – C.S. Lewis.

 There are so many things that are possible after age 60. You can consider the following:

-Run for elected office (you can run at any age, but running after 60 may be more effective due to your age)

-Try a different job (e.g., teaching), perhaps part-time or even on a volunteer basis.

-Start a business on the side or full-time—you've got plenty of life experience to share, and it's never too late to get started!

-Take a class for a new skill or new information.

-Pursue something you've always wanted to try! Whatever your age, interests, or abilities, you can find activities that will make you laugh, lose track of time, or make you feel like a kid. And many things are inexpensive or free. Start in simple ways. It's fine to try something, and it may or may not work out. That's okay. Keep exploring—there are always new opportunities, challenges, and people that can bring you joy. Decrease inhibition; get out of your own way.

Never stop learning.

Don't fret about your ability to learn something new ("old dog" syndrome)

Learning skills improve with age - In a psychological science study, 44 young adults (around age 24) and 45 older adults (around age 74) answered general questions about topics like history and geography as expected; the older adults answered more questions correctly than young adults – 41% versus 26%. But they were also more proficient in correct answers. During a surprise retest, particularly ones they had initially felt unsure about.[6]

I know a man who pursues his curiosities in a life-long way. When he wishes to know more, he reads about it, asks questions from someone knowledgeable, seeks counsel from a mentor, and takes classes.

- Books can be your new university.
- Attend in-person programs such as Osher Lifelong Learning Institute (OLLI). Usually presented at universities, OLLI provides non-credit short courses, study trips, and special events for adults aged 50+. Topics are wide-ranging in the liberal arts and sciences for the joy of learning. Programs range from one-time lectures to six-week courses. An additional benefit is to connect with others who share your interests.
- Attend online seminars. Many are free.
- Attend summer camp for seniors:

Many beautiful programs help seniors relax and enjoy themselves. Some programs offer an excellent opportunity to learn new things, meet new people, see the sights and sounds of nature, exercise in ways that strengthen muscles and tone both mind and body, cook new foods, play games with new friends or with old friends, visit museums, attend cultural events... the list goes on.

---

[6] Readers Digest, February 2016

Some of the best summer camps for adults are:

- Maine Woods Dance Camp (Farmington, Maine) August.
- Foodies CIA Boot Camp – Culinary Institute of America
- Rock 'n' Roll Fantasy Camp – Los Angeles and NYC
- Camp No Counselors (NE Pennsylvania) party camp
- Club Getaway (Kent, CT)
- Camp Halcyon (Wautoma, Wisconsin) Traditional Adult Summer Camp
- 'Camp' Camp (Portland, Maine) LGBTQ+ Summer Camp for Adults:
- Camp Wandawega (Elkhorn, Wisconsin) Nontraditional Summer Camp for Adults
- Epic Nerd Camp (Darlington, Maryland)-for sci-fi, fantasy, or gaming aficionados
- Camp Grounded – unplug, get grounded.
  Camp Grounded offers over fifty Play shops & Activities; Arts n Crafts, Yoga, Typewriters, Capture the Flag, Color Wars, Meditation, Swimming, Talent Show, Camp Dance, Campfires, Archery, Rockwall, Kickball, Stargazing, Hiking, Healthy Meals, Sing-A-Longs, Face-Painting, Analog Photography, Counselors and more.
- Santa Claus camp (New Hampshire) Learn how to be a jolly old elf!
- Mountain Playshop (Black Mountain, NC) international folk-dance weekend
- Chautauqua Institution (Chautauqua, NY) a community of artists, educators, thinkers, faith leaders dedicated to exploring the best in humanity. Each of their eight weeks of summer programs has its own theme varying from, for example, politics, philosophy, belief systems with presentations by eminent people in the field.

Volunteering:

As an older volunteer, you have some considerations that do not pertain to the stereotypical newly graduated college volunteer. For you, solid infrastructure, privacy, and a program that knows the needs of older travelers may be more critical. You might require flexible departure times, and you're undoubtedly willing to spend a little more to be more comfortable and independent. Or perhaps you require a program that will pair you with your family, spouse, or friends on a job.

1. Serve in a soup kitchen

Soup kitchens are always looking for volunteers to help serve food and cook meals. For some people, a meal at a soup kitchen may be their only food for the day. You also might be asked to greet regular patrons and welcome newcomers to the facility. A soup kitchen allows you to accept people at various life stages. It's a rewarding way to connect with the veterans, elderly folks, parents, and children in your community.

2. Aid your church

There's a good chance that churches in your community are seeking volunteer help. Churches usually host a variety of activities to bring members and non-members together. Many churches are non-profit organizations, meaning they have just a few staff members on the payroll, and rely on volunteers to assist with the rest of their activities. You can help serve, sing in the choir, organize church events, or even join a mission trip.

3. Spend time at summer camp

Maybe you've wondered, "How can I volunteer in my community but still have a lot of fun?" If so, being a summer camp counselor could be for you. Summer camps offer great opportunities for children to stay entertained until school is back in session. Not only do you get to teach the next generation of kids some valuable life skills, but you also get to enjoy the activities while teaching them. Volunteers typically help children learn new skills or information, but they also may facilitate water sports, provide meals, build campfires, play fun games, and form bonds with the children participating.

4. Assist your school

Schools are almost always looking for volunteers, and because they have a wide variety of activities, you can usually help with an activity you are interested in. If you prefer to work with adults, you can be a teacher's assistant or take tickets at a sporting event. If you want to assist young people or children, you can help serve lunch or watch recess. Volunteering at a local school is a great way to interact with younger minds and give back to your community.

5. Tutor students

If you have ever been stuck on an algebraic equation or needed help with the phrasing of an important paper, you might have wished you had a tutor to help you. Tutors help give one-on-one attention to students who need to hear the material differently. Usually, a tutor will help find an easier way for the student to interpret and learn the material. This is a great way to spark your creativity. Plus, you'll get to help students build a lifelong love of learning.

6. Mentor a child

While tutoring helps a student academically, mentoring helps a student in all aspects of life. Big Brothers Big Sisters of America connects a mentoring adult with a child who could benefit. This program, and mentorship in general, gives kids who may not have a good role model a chance to experience a healthy relationship with an adult.

7. Organize a summer reading program

Students need to remember some of the information they learned during the year throughout the summer. Summer reading programs keep their reading skills active and their minds fresh. Organizing a summer reading program is an excellent way for kids to read a book, broaden their vocabulary, and learn something new. You can share your favorite books, offer prizes to children who meet their goals, and turn the program into a friendly competition, all while teaching children the importance of reading.

8. Donate books

Donating books is a great way to give back to the children and families in your community. Old books from your childhood that you're still holding onto can help other children learn to read! Donating also helps maintain the budgets of schools and non-profit organizations that may otherwise have to purchase new books. Plus, you can free up some space on your shelf to find another book you are interested in.

9. Create a little neighborhood library.

A Little Library is most commonly a wooden box on a post; you can design your lending library however you choose! There are instructions on the internet on how to build one.

Invite people to leave a book, take a book. [For instructions, see Resources in Appendix]

10. Help out at a homeless shelter

The National Law Center on Homelessness & Poverty found that roughly 3.5 million Americans per year are sleeping in homeless shelters, transitional housing, and public places not meant for housing (bridges, bus stops, etc.) Giving your time to those going through an unfortunate stage of life can make a difference. With the older residents in a shelter, you could cook food, clean the community kitchen/common room, or teach them a new language. Alternatively, you could spend time with the children in a homeless shelter by creating an art project or making cookies.

11. Visit the elderly.

The residents of nursing homes, along with the patrons of senior centers, may not see visitors often enough and would love to have some company. Even if you don't have a family member who lives in the nursing home or goes to the senior center, you can volunteer at senior citizen events, paint nails, read books, bring baked goods, make birthday cards, and so much more. The residents will enjoy the company, and the facility will be grateful for your help! You'll probably also hear some great stories about the good old days.

12. Assist in hospitals

You don't have to have a medical background to volunteer at a hospital. You can help entertain the patients, their families, and the staff. Because a stay in a hospital is usually stressful, you can relieve some of the tension by playing an instrument in the lobby or showing off your magic tricks. You may be able to bring a smile to a sick child's face or make an exhausted nurse laugh!

13. Help in a Food Bank

A food bank is a warehouse that stores the food to be distributed to communities in need, and a food pantry delivers the food directly to the families and individuals that need it. Volunteering at a food bank or local food pantry may consist of donating food, purchasing foods with a budget, and delivering food to those in need. As a volunteer, you will help those in need with the food necessary to keep them healthy.

14 Food rescue

Also called food recovery, this is the practice of collecting fresh, edible food that would have otherwise gone to waste from restaurants, grocers, and other food establishments and distributing it to local social service agencies. It gets food to those who need it most and simultaneously reduces food waste, minimizing the huge amount that goes to landfills. Statistics show that 40% of food in this country is wasted and could feed everyone in this country four times over! https://foodrescue.us/

15. Organize a blood drive

Blood drives are essential for hospitals and their patients. Often, the patients that need blood need it urgently. If you help organize a blood drive, you could be helping to save lives! If it is accepted, the blood donated at your drive will be waiting in the blood bank for those who need it, not the other way around. Consider working with others to see if you can organize a blood drive for your school or workplace. Best of all, you'll meet new people who are just as eager to help others as you are.

16. Donate unwanted items

Some people are not fortunate enough to be able to purchase every item at the full price. These people head to shelters or thrift stores to pick up necessities for everyday life. Donating items that are unwanted or no longer used is a great way to help out your community. The gently used coats, blankets, and shoes in the back of your closet can make a big difference to others while cleaning up some of the clutter in your home. Consider donating to local charities and women's shelters.

17. Volunteer in an animal shelter

Do you want to look beyond people for contributing to your community? Consider an animal shelter, as they are always looking for volunteers to keep lively animals entertained, fed, and groomed. You may think that playing with animals cannot be considered volunteering, but helping socialize cats, dogs, and other animals to become more pleasant and friendly to humans will increase their chances for adoption.

18. Build Habitat for Humanity homes.

Help with building homes. You'll work with a skilled boss on the project. Can you pound a hammer or paint a wall? You're wanted!

19. Coach a youth sports team

Coaching a youth sports team might be the perfect volunteer opportunity if you enjoy being active or have skills in a particular sport. You'll be able to share your passion, act as a role model, and help out parents who may be too busy to take on the role themselves. You may even learn a little more about the sport yourself.

20. Gift Christmas presents

Operation Christmas Child is a great organization that allows families to put together shoe boxes of gifts to send to less fortunate children overseas. Any fun items or necessities you can pack into the shoebox can be sent over. This is a great way to help others without having to travel yourself. Common gift ideas include stuffed animals, crayons, coloring books, chapter books, and hygiene items.

21. Maintain the environment

Take a moment to imagine a beautiful local park. There may be a playground and some botanical gardens, but you probably didn't picture trash blowing through the park. Not only does this look unkempt, but it's also bad for the environment. In rural areas, you can adopt a section of the highway to clean up the roadside ditches. Planting trees in your neighborhood is another way to keep the earth clean and beautiful.

22. Package meals

Many organizations around the US make it easy for colleges, high schools, churches, and other groups to package meals for impoverished people. These meals provide proper nutrients for the children and adults who receive them. No Kid Hungry and Orphan Grain Train are some organizations working to end world hunger one meal at a time.

23. Support the Red Cross

Red Cross is an organization that helps with disaster relief, blood donations, and more. Being a Red Cross volunteer provides experience in the medical field and allows you to help those in need. The Red Cross responds to disasters nationwide and helps communities recover. It may be challenging to see devastated communities, but you could have a part in helping them recover. In addition, you may meet new friends along the way.

24. Help out in your library

– Like books? You will get to organize books while finding new books to add to your to-be-read pile. If you like working with kids, you can help young children by teaching, reading, and recommending books.

25. Support a worthy cause with fundraising.

You can set up a program in your community or establish a Go Fund Me page on the web.

26. Play at the YMCA

Volunteering at your local YMCA is one way to interact with children and act as a role model for them. Plus, you can volunteer in your area of interest. If you enjoy working out, you can teach a class in the weight room; if you enjoy playing sports, you can coach an athletic team. There are many opportunities to help young kids while staying fit.

27 Investigate volunteering through Americorps Retired and Seniors Volunteer program.

Make a positive difference in your community. AmeriCorps Seniors volunteers serve with organizations dedicated to helping others.

https://americorps.gov/serve/americorps-seniors

28 Volunteer to participate in Alzheimer's research.

By volunteering for a clinical study or clinical trial, you can become a partner in helping researchers discover new ways to potentially diagnose, treat, and prevent Alzheimer's disease and related dementias.   www.alzheimers.gov/clinical-trials

So now you know a few great ways to get involved in your community and make a difference. What are you waiting for? By picking one of the skills or interests on this list, you can turn your passion into a community service project that makes an impact. Many organizations will even help you create your way to give back.

There is no such thing as an act too small. Even if you don't think one community service project will make much of an impact, it might be exactly what someone needs now.

Fun Activities

- Teach yourself to play a recorder flute or a keyboard.
- Attend cultural events: museums, theaters, and concerts.
- Join a book club or start one!
- Senior centers and community groups offer a variety of activities, such as fitness classes, arts and crafts, and social events.
- Take up pickleball.
- Take up archery.
- Join or start an amateur club for model airplanes, improv, photography, or radio.
- Try disk golf or amateur Frisbee.
- Explore virtual reality (see next chapter--Technology)
- Try writing poems.
- Write a memoir.
- Write essays.
- Write a children's book.
- Take a painting class.
- Create a labyrinth (See Appendix)
- Go Forest Bathing.
- Create an interesting collection of something. (Be careful of this one –you don't want to add items when you may be at the point in your life of trying to "pare down") Some examples of petite collections: shot glasses, souvenir spoons, patches, and magnets.
- Butterfly Tree guest book. Find an interesting branch that branches out like a tree. Print paper butterflies (grab some graphics from the internet). Have guests at your house sign the back of a butterfly with their name and date. Glue a

short piece of thread to the butterfly and attach it to a branch.

- Take up gardening in small spaces or pots
- Learning online - examples:
  - ➤ Learn the game of bocci or pétanque.
  - ➤ Identify mushrooms.
  - ➤ Take up gardening.
    https://local.aarp.org/gardening/events *from AARP Virtual Community Center)*
- Profit from the many benefits of exploring a new language A second language uses both sides of the brain. Acquiring a new language also helps to stave off cognitive decline and mental aging. Recent research shows that multilingual adults experienced the first signs of Alzheimer's and dementia at a later age compared to monolinguals.
- Take up wood carving. You can get started by watching any number of YouTube videos, such as Wood Carving for Beginners –Basics & Tips
  www.youtube.com/watch?v=axiGtO48_KE.

Join an interest group

You can join a group. Look online to see what kinds of local groups there may be, reflecting an interest you already have, or one you'd like to learn about.

Joining groups for older adults can prove beneficial. It improves emotional, intellectual, and physical wellness. Overall wellness in all these areas is key to getting and staying healthy as a person ages. Being involved in social activities can help stave off isolation and loneliness – two issues seniors may face if they aren't socially engaged.

Social activities allow individuals to connect with others while also improving their mood. Classes, lectures, and concerts are all chances to interact with others and boost one's mood.

General Support Groups

Not all senior support organizations are specialized. Some may be general groups for seniors in the local neighborhood. Seniors in these groups typically discuss the challenges of aging and sympathize with others in similar situations. These support groups can be an excellent way to interact with others of the same generation. In some instances, senior support groups will plan group outings and events, which can also serve as a form of social interaction.

Stay curious and stay inspired.

Many have claimed that if you practice "manifesting," that is, focusing your thought and energy on what you want in your life, you can attract it.

"Life is like riding a bicycle, and you must keep moving to keep your balance." -Albert Einstein.

I can seek involvement in _____
to connect to my community.

> 9 <
Technology

"Technology, like art, is a soaring exercise of the human imagination." – Daniel Bell

"Technology should improve your life... Not become your life " – Billy Cox.

This his chapter will touch on some helpful aspects of using the technology available to us today. Of course, it would take  more than a whole book to cover topics in this area, but we're touching on some. The first section deals with various devices that enable you to do more with less and connect with your friends, companions, and loved ones.

Two interesting facts: the Internet was born Jan 1 1983. The Worldwide Web (www) was launched in 1989.

Reader, you may be tech savvy enough to skip over most of this, but for those less familiar, we'll define a few terms:

Podcast: A podcast is an audio program made available in digital format for download over the Internet. For example, an episodic series of digital audio files (like interviews or discussions) that a user can download to a personal device to listen to at a time of their choosing.

Blog: A website that allows users to reflect, share opinions, and discuss various topics in the form of an online journal; readers may comment on posts.

Cloud: virtual servers on the internet, allowing your digital files to be stored there, instead of on your physical computer.

Cookie: A small bit of data that is deposited onto your device when visiting most websites, used as a means of identifying you. Cookies are how your browser can present advertising to you based on previously visited sites.

HTML (HyperText Markup Language) - the standard language used to create web pages.

Operating system: An OS is software that manages processes on a computer allowing programs and applications to run.

VPN: A virtual private network used to connect to a private network across a public network, enabling users to send and receive data securely from anywhere in the world as if they're directly connected to the private network.

File types: jpg, gif, pdf, txt --*jpg* and *gif* are graphics or picture files; *pdf* is the file type used by Adobe Reader and is a format for the transmission of a multimedia document that is not intended to be edited further; it includes formatting and often graphics (pictures.); *txt* files are strictly text, without formatting.

Computer spreadsheets:

A spreadsheet is a tool to store, manipulate and analyze data. Data in a spreadsheet is organized in a series of rows and columns and can be searched, sorted, calculated, and used in various charts and graphs.

A specialized spreadsheet application is required to make an electronic spreadsheet. Microsoft Excel is the most popular spreadsheet software, but other applications exist.

Some of the popular uses of Excel sheets are:

<u>Budgeting:</u> Spreadsheets are great for creating and tracking budgets. You can use formulas to automatically calculate totals and track expenses over time.

Address list: Organize by name, address, city, state, zip, and many other useful categories in the columns, such as children's names, notes, and 'send Christmas card?'. This can be the source to merge into a file that will print mailing labels.

Other lists can be of birthdays, donations, books you've read or borrowed or lent, passwords (see passwords below),

Record keeping: Spreadsheets can be used to keep track of any type of record, including financial transactions, donations given, medical records. You can use them to store and organize data in a way that is easy to search and retrieve.

Packing list – Very handy. It lists all items you want to pack, including clothes and accessories for winter, summer, etc. Put an "x" for the ones you want in an adjacent column, then filter on the x's. Print it and use it so as not to forget anything!

Managing passwords

Programs often offer to create a strong password for you.

A password manager can be a "bucket" to keep track of <u>all</u> your passwords. Some password managers: 1Password, Dashlane, Keeper, or KeePass XC, Panda, NordPass, RoboForm, StickyPassword, and Kaspersky. You type in your password only once. Then, you can log in from all your devices without retyping it. Also, it stores the passwords securely, lets you generate secure ones, log in with a single click, and RoboForm can even complete long online checkout forms. RoboForm works across all major browsers and devices (from iPhone to Android devices to your computer).

If you don't want to use a password manager, creating a different password for each application, account, etc., may seem daunting. Still, you can have a way to create different ones that are, nonetheless, relatively easy to remember.

A spreadsheet can include your site address, login name, email address (if you use different ones for different applications or businesses, etc.), password in abbreviated form (for security), and date first used or updated.

Communications programs

You can use technology to talk with friends and relatives or even play interactive games with them. You can use your home computer, or you can use your cell phone. Your cell phone, tablet, and computer have many online chat programs. Most of you've probably already heard of FaceTime, Google Chat, MSN Messenger (just bought by Skype), WhatsApp, and many others that are free for basic use. It would be good to research the various programs and find the one that fits your needs. If you have a lot of friends who use various mobile devices, they will most likely be able to use them.

Various places on the internet provide people with information on how to use specific technology tools and devices. These can be found in print, on the web, and YouTube. You can also find classes at a local college, university, or library that will help teach you how to use these different tools and devices. It would benefit you to know these things because they will come in handy when you need them in the future.

Virtual meetings - one on one or group:

Zoom combines cloud video conferencing, simple online meetings, and cross-platform group chat. It is free for 40-minute sessions; offers a monthly subscription for longer meetings. ★ it is rated above 4 stars by Forbes.

Google Meet: Google's latest replacement for Hangouts ★ rated above 4 stars by Forbes.

Google Hangouts ... upgraded to **Google Chat**. Use Google Chat to message a person or group.

Skype, a telecommunications application operated by Skype Technologies (Microsoft), is best known for VoIP-based videotelephony, videoconferencing, and voice calls. It also has instant messaging and file transfer and answers questions based on new AI technology.

Zoho Meeting - online meetings with real-time audio, video, and screen sharing at zero cost.

Microsoft Teams - for chats, meetings, calls, and collaboration

Calls with video: FaceTime is a video-telephony product developed by Apple Inc. FaceTime is available on iPhones and Macs with a forward-facing camera. It is possible to join a FaceTime call from an Android or Windows device with Wi-Fi or on the web. Usually for person-to-person calls, but it can be used for group chats.

WhatsApp, which is accessible on phones all over the world, provides messaging and calling. While it mostly works on cell phones, WhatsApp also works over Wi-Fi and 4G.

Meetup - a social media platform for hosting and organizing in-person and virtual activities, gatherings, and events for people and communities of similar interests, hobbies, and professions.

Other helpful tasks via internet

File transfers: Cloud storage services are increasingly common. For example, Dropbox started as an online place to store and share files. It has expanded its file-sharing service from cloud storage to include personal photos, videos, and music. Google Drive also offers free cloud storage for documents of all kinds under the "Google Drive" brand name. These and other such services can be done through a web browser without installing any software on a computer system.

Online services

You can use technology to find places to shop, eat and stay when traveling. You can find such places on the internet or on your cell phone.

You can also make reservations for these services through the internet, computer, or mobile device. You no longer need to call airlines or hotels directly when you want to make a reservation.

When you have flight reservations, you can receive up-to-the-minute information on gates, departure time changes, and more.

An assortment of sites provide information about events happening in your area and worldwide. Some provide daily news about sports, weather, national news, politics, etc., while others will give you information about art exhibits, concerts, performances, and other entertainment events. Some of these sites are free; others require a membership fee. Research and find ones that provide the information you are interested in.

Virtual reality

Virtual reality (VR) technology has become very popular in the past few years. You can use a virtual reality headset with your home computer to play games like flight simulators. You can also use a VR headset with an Android phone to play games and watch movies in virtual reality.

New digital worlds await you in the fun and entertainment VR can provide. It can be a great way to experience immersive experiences –a walk through Paris or meeting a mastodon!

Here are the steps to follow:

1) Choose a VR headset, one that suits your needs and fits your budget. Among the several options available are standalone devices like the Oculus Quest 2 to PC-based systems like the HTC Vive and the Valve Index. Research the different options and choose the one that is right for you.

2) Set up the hardware: After choosing your VR headset, follow the instructions to set it up, which will typically involve connecting the headset to a PC or a gaming console. You will likely need to install the necessary software or drivers and set up any sensors or cameras required for tracking.

3) Set up the area where you plan to use your VR equipment. This could involve clearing furniture out of a room or marking out a safe area with some boundary markers. The manufacturer's guidelines will likely give you suggestions for setting up your play space.

4) Choose your games and experiences. Available VR games and experiences range from immersive adventures to puzzle games and educational experiences. Have fun choosing the ones that interest you or try something new! Download them into your VR headset.

5) Now, you can start playing. Don't forget to breathe and drink water!

Smartwatches

Smartwatches can be incredibly useful tools for staying connected, staying active, and keeping track of your health and fitness.

1. <u>Fitness tracking</u>: Many smartwatches come with built-in fitness tracking features such as step counting, heart rate monitoring, and calorie tracking. These features can help you stay motivated and track progress towards your fitness goals.

2. <u>Notifications</u>: Smartwatches can display notifications for incoming calls, text messages, and emails, allowing you to stay connected without having to constantly check your phone.

3. <u>Voice assistants</u>: Many smartwatches now come with built-in voice assistants like Siri, Alexa, or Google Assistant, allowing you to use voice commands to perform tasks like setting reminders, making calls, or checking the weather.

4. <u>Mobile payments</u>: Some smartwatches support mobile payments, allowing you to make purchases at stores without having to pull out your wallet.

5. <u>GPS</u>: Smartwatches can also include GPS (Global Positioning System) functionality, allowing you to track your location and navigate while on the go.

6. <u>Music control</u>: With a smartwatch, you can control music playback on your phone without having to take it out of your pocket.

7. <u>Sleep tracking</u>: Many smartwatches can also track your sleep patterns, giving you insight into the quality and duration of your sleep.

8. <u>Health monitoring</u>: Some smartwatches include health monitoring features such as blood pressure monitoring or ECG monitoring, which can help you keep track of your health and detect potential issues early on.

Scams

There are some disadvantages or downsides to modern technology. Scamming is one of the most common of them.

People will try to find ways to scam you for your money or in other ways that can damage you.

Avoiding scams

There are numerous scams, and it's important to be aware of them to avoid becoming a victim. Below are some common scams and tips on how to avoid them:

Never click on links or attachments asking you to confirm personal or payment information.

Phishing Scams: These are scams where an individual is sent an email or a text message that looks like it is from a legitimate source, such as a bank or an online store, asking for personal information. To avoid this type of scam, be wary of any unsolicited requests for personal information, and do not click on links from unknown sources. Always contact the company directly, using the number or website on your credit card or statement, or by looking up the number yourself.

'Thanks for your order' scam: An invoice arrives via email saying your account (credit card, etc.) has been charged for your subscription to a service (computer protection, technical help, etc.) and providing a number to call if you feel the charge is "in error." Please look at the sender's email address; it does not look official, often coming from another country or with a name misspelling. Delete the email, or perhaps even report it to the legitimate company.

Tech support scams: These scams involve someone pretending to be a tech support specialist and offering to fix your computer for a fee. To avoid this scam, only trust tech support from reputable companies, and be cautious of unsolicited tech support offers.

Online dating scams: These scams involve someone creating a fake profile on a dating site and tricking their victim into giving them money. To avoid this scam, be cautious of people asking for money and never send money to someone you've never met.

Grandparent scam This is a type of telephone scam that targets older individuals, specifically grandparents. The scammer will call and pretend to be the victim's grandchild, claiming to be in trouble and in need of money immediately. The scammer will often say they have been in a car accident or arrested and need money to get out of jail or pay medical bills. The scammer will typically ask the victim to wire money or buy gift cards and provide the card information over the phone.

The scammer will usually play on the victim's emotions by pretending to be upset and crying and may ask the victim not to tell his or her parents or other family members about the situation. This can make the victim feel like they must act quickly and not ask too many questions.

To avoid falling victim to this scam, it's important to confirm the identity of the person calling by asking specific questions that only the grandchild would know, such as their middle name or pet's name. Additionally, it's important to resist the pressure to act quickly and to verify the situation with other family members before sending money. Finally, wiring money or providing gift card information over the phone is a red flag and should be avoided.

Investment scams: These scams involve someone promising to make you rich quickly through investing. To avoid this scam, be wary of promises of high returns with little risk and only invest with reputable companies.

Cryptocurrency scams: Cryptocurrency, such as Bitcoin, is a type of digital currency that generally exists only electronically. You usually use your phone, computer, or a cryptocurrency ATM to buy cryptocurrency. Cryptocurrency accounts are not backed by any government. Cryptocurrency held in accounts is not insured by a government like the U.S. for dollars deposited into an FDIC insured bank account. The value of a cryptocurrency can change rapidly, even changing by the hour.

No legitimate business is going to demand you send cryptocurrency in advance – not to buy something, and not to protect your money. That's always a scam.

Only scammers will guarantee profits or big returns. Don't trust people who promise you can quickly and easily make money in the crypto markets.

Charity scams: These scams involve someone posing as a charity and asking for donations. To avoid this type of scam, only donate to charities you know and trust, and be cautious of unsolicited requests for donations. Use Charity Navigator or another charity "watchdog" to determine whether a charity is using donations wisely.

Overall, it's important to be cautious and research before giving out personal information or money to someone you don't know or trust. If the payee asks to be paid in gift cards, that's a big "red flag"!

Don't share too much info: You don't want to share too much information on social media sites like Facebook or Twitter. Avoid sharing your address, phone number, or anything other than your name and location. Also, avoid posting pictures of yourself where people can see where you live. Remember that people other than yourself could also save these pictures online. You are sharing your personal information with the whole world.

Artificial Intelligence or AI

We are on the threshold of AI being used in many ways. A few of the many:

1. AI-powered virtual assistants such as Siri, Alexa, and Google Assistant can help you with various tasks, from setting reminders to providing weather updates and even controlling smart home devices.

2. Social media platforms use AI to suggest content you might be interested in based on your previous activity and behavior. They also use AI to identify and remove inappropriate or harmful content.

3. Customer service: Many companies use AI-powered chatbots to handle customer inquiries and support requests, freeing human agents to handle more complex issues.

4. Navigation: GPS and mapping apps use AI to update real-time traffic and suggest the fastest route to your destination based on current conditions.

5. Healthcare: AI is used in medical diagnosis and treatment planning, such as identifying tumors in medical images and predicting disease progression.

6. Financial services: AI is used to detect fraud and provide personalized financial advice to customers.

7. Entertainment: AI-powered recommendations are used to suggest movies, TV shows, music, and books that you might enjoy based on your past viewing or listening history.

8. Transportation: AI is used in self-driving cars to detect obstacles, recognize traffic signals, and make decisions about navigating roads and intersections.

9. Translation AI can transcribe audio into text in many possible languages, then translate and transcribe the audio into English.

10. Respond to questions. AI can be used to scour the web for answers to questions, then formulate an appropriate response. Three AI conversational or large language model (LLM) programs are capturing attention: OpenAI's GPT -4, Anthropic's Claude, and Google's Bard. Poe is also a free AI chat app by Quora.

11. Some AI programs can do programming or even create poetry. Here's a poem created in a flash by ChatGPT:

In the age of AI,
Our world is changing fast.
Machines that think and learn
Are becoming unsurpassed.
From virtual assistants to self-driving cars
To personalized medicine and financial stars.
AI is reshaping our daily lives
In ways that we cannot even surmise
As we embrace this new frontier
Let's remember to keep what we hold dear,
And use these tools to improve and enhance
The world we live in, and give it a chance,
So let us welcome the age of AI
And use its power to simplify.
And with each innovation and creation
Let's strive to build a better civilization.

Not exactly Pulitzer-Prize quality, but it rhymes!

An   idea   from   this   chapter   I   intend   to   use

_____

> 10 <
Discovering New Places

"Not all those who wander are lost." – J.R.R. Tolkien

"Oh, the places you'll go." – Dr. Seuss

At this point in your life, you can now take a global perspective on life. You have seen many political and cultural changes, including the fall of the Berlin Wall and the birth of Eastern Europe's "New Europe." You have seen how regimes can crumble in what used to seem like stable countries. You may well have attended Woodstock or other music festivals back in the day.

The good news is that it's never too late to learn something new or embark on a new venture. You may want to speak several languages. You may want to travel more or participate more in your local community. You may want to emigrate to another country if that option still beckons. The world is full of possibilities for you!

You may travel with your spouse or even your grandchildren at this age. Exploring new destinations can create beautiful memories and strong bonds. Or you might like to travel with a friend.

You can start by visiting close-by places, i.e., a new area of your town or city. You then go on to a slightly longer distance location, e.g., a nearby state or province. You could visit a farm that allows you to pick your fruits, vegetables, and flowers. Whether spring, summer, or fall, you may be able to find places that offer pick-your-own berries, flowers, or tree fruits such as cherries or apples --a great activity for older adults to enjoy with family and companions. Besides you are young enough to enjoy the countryside!

Have you ever tried strawberries picked right from the plants or an apple straight from the tree? Find farms in your area with the "you pick" option. Several farms provide hay rides out into the orchard. Then in December, you may be able to go to a tree farm to select a live-cut Christmas tree.

You could visit a museum and learn history, science, or art. You can become a tourist in your town, state, or province. There are many attractions within a short drive from your home! You can go to your city hall and learn about all the museums and theatres in your area.

In your state, you can plan to travel a scenic byway. Scenic drives can be some of the best mini-trips to connect with family, with benefits beyond the delightful destination. Your state Travel & Tourism Bureau can likely send you a fat guide to trips and attractions in your state. (Or, for that matter, get one from any state you'd like to visit.)

Seniors who travel with grandchildren benefit from an improved relationship with their grown and married children. Planning a journey with elderly family members can also remind us to slow down and appreciate what we have.

Planning your dream vacation isn't hard. You can visit websites and travel blogs and read about the places you want to visit. Planning your trip can help you immerse yourself in the culture you are studying so that you will feel very much at home when you return. You could also hire a guide to show you your favorite places in your hometown or elsewhere.

Recommended travel companies

Travel agencies can greatly help in planning your vacations. Here are a few good ones:

Intrepid Travel

Intrepid Travel embraces adventurers of all ages and does not just cater to the younger demographic. Travelers often find companionship with others of similar interests. Their new active packages, featuring walking, trekking, biking, and multi-activity trips, appeal to senior explorers aged 50 and above. However, these tours are designed to require just a "general level of health and fitness and are enjoyable rather than being a relentless test of endurance.

Road Scholar

For many years, Road Scholar--previously known to lifetime learners and travelers as Elderhostel--has offered educational tours across all 50 states and more than 100 countries. While the average guest is 72, the ages range from 50 to 90. On these senior-oriented journeys, activity levels vary from easy-going classroom-focused sessions to physically strenuous options such as the "Outdoor: Challenging" programs catering to the adventurous.

Smithsonian Journeys

Smithsonian Journeys caters to seniors who prefer spending extended periods at a single location. You can delve deeper into a destination with Smithsonian Journeys' Classic and Active programs or their "Living In" program. The latter lets travelers live like locals in Italy, France, and Spain over three weeks while availing of expert tour guides and structured learning opportunities. This is a unique combination of experiential travel and educational enrichment.

Backroads

Backroads specializes in active leisure trips, understanding that outdoor sports remain a lifelong passion for many. Their cycling, hiking, and multi-sport tours offer a range of activities from vigorous to relaxed, an excellent range for senior travel. The trip may include e-bikes and support vehicles in most cycling tours for added ease. Their new Dolce Tempo rides offer an enjoyable, adventurous experience without demanding too much physically.

Trafalgar

Trafalgar, a respected name in the travel industry, primarily serves guests between 50 and 71. With skilled tour planning and local expertise, Trafalgar creates travel experiences that are innovative yet comfortable. Trafalgar has the industry's first health manager, ensuring adherence to health standards in light of recent safety concerns.

Overseas Adventure Travel (OAT)

OAT specifically caters to travelers aged 50 and over, providing diverse, structured tours for senior explorers. OAT offers extended trips of two weeks or longer, with options for pre- and post-trip extensions. You can choose energy and mobility levels to meet your physical level. Solo travelers can also avail themselves of no or low single surcharges. This year, 92% of its 30,000 individual slots will have no surcharge.

Your travel solution might lie in a multigenerational family vacation package catering to everyone's needs.

Numerous great family resorts, family-friendly glamping destinations, and child-centric vacation spots in the United States, Canada, and the Caribbean cater to every age, from the youngest grandkids to the adult generations and elderly members of the family.

Some ideas for multi-generational travel destinations

The following places are a sample of some outstanding places offering a mix of adventure, tranquility, and a range of experiences, to give you some ideas.

1. Chilco Lake Bear Camp, British Columbia

Formerly a fishing and hunting lodge, Bear Camp is now a luxury safari-style campground suited to active seniors who love the outdoors and adventurous families. Formerly a fishing and hunting camp, it is now a tented camp, "glamping"-style. Summer activities at Bear Camp include rafting, hiking, biking, fishing, kayaking, canoeing, paddling, horseback riding, archery, rock climbing, and ice climbing. There are bear sightings in September and October. At Glacier Camp, you can camp for the night at the foot of the glacier.

2. Brasada Ranch Powell Butte, Oregon

The family-friendly Brasada Ranch resort in Central Oregon offers multigenerational living arrangements on nearly 2,000 acres. You can choose ranch house suites or cabins,

Dude ranch activities include pony rides for younger children; for others, horseback rides through the high desert. Relax in two outdoor pools, a spa, and an indoor kiddie pool. For golf enthusiasts, there's a course to play. Age-appropriate activities include astronomy, paint kits, puzzles, strength training and yoga classes.

3. Kimpton Seafire Resort and Spa, Grand Cayman, Cayman Islands

Step onto Seven Mile Beach, ranked among the top beaches worldwide. Right on these shores is the Kimpton Seafire Resort and Spa, where you can indulge in thermal mud body treatments and deep relaxation massages with Caribbean Sea Salts, among other options. Once rejuvenated, select from a variety of water sports on offer. Grand Cayman offers over 200 diving locations, underground caves, botanical gardens, forest trails, museums, and more. For children aged 4-8 and 9-12, Camp Seafire offers daily themed programs.

4. The Broadmoor, Colorado Springs, Colorado

At the foot of the Colorado Rockies is the AAA Five-Diamond Broadmoor. Select from various pools: an indoor pool or the impressive heated 11,000-square-foot infinity outdoor pool with two water slides, two 14-person whirlpools, and even a kiddie pool.

You have many room styles from which to choose among the 800 rooms on the property: Estate House, a lavish Gatsby-style 12,000 sq ft, five-bedroom private historic mansion; the sophisticated brownstones with gourmet kitchens and private wine cellars; or perhaps the cottages that offer panoramic views of the East golf course and Cheyenne Mountain. In addition, there are the wilderness properties—a complete dude ranch with horses and a lake; luxury cabins with hot tubs at an elevation of 3,000 feet (Camp Cloud); or the cabins and lodge at the Fly-Fishing Camp.

Activities include: golfing, tennis, pickleball, bowling, hiking, mountain biking, boating, canoeing, or thrilling ziplining. Games, including shuffleboard, a pool table, foosball, Xbox, PlayStation, and Wii Adventures, moderate hiking, crossing a suspension bridge, and performing a controlled 180-foot rappel. Consider a leisurely, less strenuous walk with a naturalist or boating on Cheyenne Lake.

A range of activities for kids aged eight to 12 includes arts and crafts, games, movies, falconry, storytelling, outdoor recreation, educational activities, and field trips to the Cheyenne Zoo.

5. Hyatt Regency Grand Reserve, Rio Grande, Puerto Rico

This reserve offers all-suite, bungalow-style accommodations in PR's sole tropical rainforest.

Enjoy two 18-hole world-class golf courses and soothing massages at the on-site full-service spa, and relax on the pristine beach or at three resort pools, including a lagoon-style pool, and have fun at the floating waterpark just off the beach.

Discover the waterfalls of El Yunque National Rainforest just a few miles away. If you're up for it, kayak in one of the island's three bioluminescent bays, go ziplining, or visit the historic 18th-century fortress, Castillo San Cristóbal, in San Juan. Venture into the foothills on ATVs. At Carabalí Rainforest Park or horseback ride along riverside trails through the rainforestAt the end of the day, enjoy delicious meals at any of the five on-site dining establishments watching the beautiful sunset.

6. Whiteface Lodge, Lake Placid, New York

In the woodlands at Lake Placid, the Whiteface Lodge is an all-suite, AAA Four Diamond resort combining handcrafted Adirondack style with luxury. Like the outdoors? There's hiking and skiing. Free amenities include a 56-seat movie theater, a game room with a two-lane bowling alley, a fishing pond, nightly s'mores, and an ice-skating rink. You can also enjoy an award-winning spa. Additionally, for children aged three to ten. the free children's club, Kamp Kanu with educational activities like science experiments, arts and crafts, and is open seven days a week during summer.

7. Four Seasons Resort, Peninsula Papagayo, Guanacaste, Costa Rica

The Four Seasons Resort at the Peninsula Papagayo in Costa Rica offers an array of experiences for every age group; the resort offers restful views of the Pacific Ocean and serves as an ideal launchpad for unforgettable family travel adventures --ziplining, hiking a volcano, surfing, or exploring on an electric bike.

Swim in one of the four pools or a rejuvenating treatment at the spa. Kids will be entertained with various activities like scavenger hunts, dance classes, guided nature hikes, or snorkeling. Meals for kids under five are complimentary.

Other travel ideas: You can get narrated travel videos online on YouTube. They will give you a good idea of what kind of weather, food, and activities to expect.

Be sure to plan to take videos of your travel adventure. Think about using a GoPro camera to go beyond your cell phone camera.

Start planning your next adventure today!

Two places I'd like to go are _____ and_____.

A travel adventure I'd like to plan is:

_____.

> 11 <
Downsizing:

"Do your stuff and the things around you represent who you are today, or who you were in the past?" – The Unclutter Angel

One of life's most challenging and emotionally draining transitions is what to do with your stuff when you move or downsize. This important project may include selling or donating items and checking with family members. Downsizing should be done deliberately, thoughtfully, and at your own pace.

Involve your family: ask your children (now adults, likely which items are meaningful to them, and give them each a turn at selecting those things which have meaning for them, and either give them now or write down their wishes, so it will be decided in advance.

If it is done correctly, there are a lot of benefits to downsizing. You get to your home looking the way you always wanted it to look. You spend less time, money, and energy keeping it up or worrying about it not looking its best. You may find that you can move into a smaller home if you have sold all your "stuff,".

I know a woman, who when she moved, took only what she could take with her in her SUV!

Decluttering:

Clutter is postponed decisions.

Few of us are minimalists, so you've probably got a lot of stuff.

Let excess go to allow room for new opportunities to move in. That's true of more than just the stuff in your home.

A cluttered house can make you irritable and raise your stress levels. You will feel more relaxed and calmer after decluttering your home.

When you declutter your house, you may discover many hidden treasures. If they no longer appear to be keepable treasures, hold a yard sale to boost your family's holiday money.

Where to sell your stuff and realize a little profit? Yes, there are yard sales/garage sales. They take a LOT of time to prepare, but sometimes someone will come at the end of the day and make an offer on everything left—low, but you get rid of what you didn't want anyway.

Other channels:

- Local online sales sites – Craigslist, Nextdoor, OfferUp, Facebook Marketplace.
- eBay – You can sell auction style, or state a "Buy it Now" price.
- Consignment stores – nice clothing, nice furniture
- Pawnshops - most are reputable (tightly regulated)
- Auction houses - especially some with an online component for maximum exposure
- Estate sales – can be treated like a yard sale because most buyers are looking for a bargain.
- Local Classifieds – this used to be about the only place. Now it may be a less effective place to sell items than the rest of this list.

You will transform your home from a place of accumulated stuff to one in which each object has been considered for its usefulness and beauty. This will help you create a meaningful uncluttered environment that reflects your life now.

For some folks, it's all about the tales associated with the items. "It wasn't the things I'd saved that were important; it was the stories that went with them that gave them meaning," Bob Stein said in a Ted Talk. Could using the objects to share the stories be the seed of a new ritual, a rite of passage?

Paper can be a huge problem and tends to pile up incredibly. The paper beast has three heads: miscellaneous papers, documents, and files.

What one area in your home stresses you out? That's a good place to start decluttering!

What to toss:

1. Anything that adds no worth

You should ask yourself, "How might my life be better with less?" This can assist you in understanding why you want to downsize, which is highly personal.

2. Items that have been damaged

Do you have a favorite mug that has chipped or a necklace that has come apart? It's time to let go. "Be honest about what items are damaged and toss them,"

3. Expired items

This includes medicines, meals, and cosmetics. Old makeup can damage skin and eyes.

4. Does it trigger negative emotions?

If something doesn't make you happy, let it go. Sell it, give it away, toss it.

5. An abandoned pastime

Be honest about which hobbies you've abandoned and dispose of any related materials. Get rid of that yarn you will never knit. Don't keep brushes and paint for a painting pastime you will never pursue. And if you stumble across hobby materials and want to complete the project, go ahead and do so. Completion of a project can qualify as decluttering and is a beneficial mindset shift.

6. Photographs and paper

Allow yourself to eliminate duplicate, similar, or blurry photographs; coupons, bills, and statements you can get online; outdated newspapers, magazines, and articles torn from magazines. You can copy photos to create digital versions, which have the added benefit of being shareable.

• Ask yourself questions about that pile of greeting cards. Is the card's substance vital to me? Do I adore the card's design?

Assuming your grandson or most loved niece sent something that pulls at your heart, you can make it into digital form on your PC or put it in a collection; however, first ask yourself, "Will I look at it again?" Would I miss it in the future? Release it with a "goodbye," then throw it away.

• If a photo is included with the card, is it a "prize-winner"? Do I know all the people in it? Is it a wonderful memory?

Consider committing a case to hard-to-leave-behind things like letters and photos.

7. Items from a past phase

If you're retired, pack up most of your professional clothes and office supplies. If you don't have a dog anymore and don't plan on getting a new one, give yourself permission to get rid of the dog bed, bowl, and leash. You're defining your life for now, not for back then.

8. JIC

Don't keep something thinking, "just in case", it might be useful in the future. You can probably replace it if there is ever a need. If you don't use it, don't keep it

Swedish Death Cleaning: *döstädning*

Swedish death cleaning is organizing and decluttering your house before you die to reduce the burden on your loved ones after your death.

Now is a good time to determine what's essential.

This decluttering philosophy can apply to many aspects of your house. It is more than just wiping down surfaces or doing a deep clean—at its core, Swedish death cleaning is about choosing what to keep and discard. There are four categories: the pared-down "keep" pile, a pile to donate (or possibly sell), a pile to throw away, and "not sure yet".

Clothing First

Sort out what fits and doesn't or what you once liked and now don't.

Clean up by Size

Begin with furniture and other things that occupy the most space. From that point, you can work your direction down to more modest items and individual keepsakes — consider designating a special box or a case for hard-to-leave-behind things like letters and photos.

As you clean up, don't get distracted by whether something flashes satisfaction (this isn't the Konmari technique). In the kitchen, for example, consider the items you use daily, frequently, once or twice a year, or never. You know what happens to items in that last category!

Think Computerized

When we bite the dust, our friends and family go through more than just our belongings. You want to consider the computerized mess they'll likewise have to figure out, which implies ensuring they have login abilities for things like internet-based ledgers and other significant wellsprings of data. While doing this, consider taking an evening (It may take longer!) to clean up your hard drive and work area — a wreck nobody anticipates managing.

Rather than being encircled by arbitrary articles, the things you keep are instilled with more profound and long-lasting significance.

Ultimately, there's no correct method for doing Swedish demise cleaning. However long you're paring down the messiness around your home and encircling yourself with the most significant fundamentals, you're not just making things simpler for your friends and family — you're carrying on with a more purposeful life right now.

You don't want to undertake this process when you are sick or in any form of distress. This can also affect the time you have to complete this task.

An area where I can focus my de-cluttering attention first is

_____

> 12 <
Senior Living Considerations

For some people, a retirement residence provides the best of both worlds: a supportive community of seniors and access to the amenities of modern living in one location. Others prefer their own  home with assistance from caregivers when needed. Most Americans want options — and most communities provide them to seniors who invest in their future by planning for what's next.

Living Options for Seniors

Staying in your own home:

The advantages of staying in your home include feeling secure and comfortable, having your own space, making it your home, and eventually selling it when you're ready. You can hire assistance as needed with chores and medical attention. If you have the money, you can be more independent than in an assisted-living or a nursing home. But if another patient in the house needs help with caregiving, moving to an assisted living center may make more sense.

Have a movable residence:

You can even consider giving up a house in a fixed place and take to the road in an RV or motor home and go to an RV park. This can open up possibilities of seeing new places!

There are even people who live from cruise ship to cruise ship!

Levels of Senior Living Communities

Independent Living (cottages, apartments)

Independent living aims to blend the familiar comforts of home with the excitement of new experiences and more. After settling into a Senior Lifestyle Community, those who live there frequently ask why they did not relocate sooner. Examples of independent-living residences are individual cottages or apartments in larger buildings.

Assisted Living

Programs supplement the Independent Living program by providing additional support. The Assisted Living Services are intended for persons who appreciate their freedom but could benefit from assistance with daily activities. Senior Living's professional staff are there to assist with any need; they can help with washing, clothing, and medication.

Continuing Care Retirement Community

A CCRC community offers several different senior living options on one campus. As necessary to the individual, a person may progress from independent living to assisted living to even memory care as these best suit the senior individual's requirements.

Memory care

Alzheimer's and other forms of dementia take a severe toll on those suffering from the disease and their loved ones. This care level has dedicated specialists who work with residents, their families, and staff to ensure comprehensive and personalized treatment, individually assisting cognitive and social skills. Memory care residents live in communities that balance safety and participation in shared spaces and external courtyards.

The attributes in common of these facilities

Every community has its own distinct identity, but even at the most basic level of care, each group of care typically supplements a variety of amenities, such as a delicious dining experience, stimulating and engaging life enrichment programs, optional routine laundry and housekeeping services, transportation to local attractions and physicians, and so much more.

Other types of care facilities

• Short-term care

Short-term care offers a short-term supportive environment with rehabilitation or respite care for those not quite ready for Assisted living or even Independent living. Short-term care services can range from 12–48 hours, depending on the need and level of care residents require. This can be especially beneficial when an elder requires immediate medical attention or suffers from an unexpected illness and needs assistance for recovery.

• Skilled nursing

Skilled nursing care helps get people back on their feet and into their daily lives. Skilled nursing can help with various conditions, including physical therapy and recovery from surgery or simply moving back into an Independent Living or Assisted Living environment.

This level of care is usually a short-term solution, and residents generally stay no more than 90–120 days, depending on the extent of their condition. Residents receive physical care and participate in rehabilitation therapy to help regain strength, balance, and mobility to resume home life safely and independently. In addition, Skilled Nursing Care gives the family a chance to rest so they can focus on other aspects of life.

• Respite Care:

Respite care allows a primary caregiver to take a much-needed break from the demands of caring for a sick, elderly, or disabled family member. Respite care can be provided in the comfort of your home, day-care centers, or residential or nursing facilities offering overnight stays.

Whether for a few hours a week or for an extended vacation, obtaining respite care can assist in lightening a load of family caregiving while also relieving stress, restoring energy, and promoting balance in your life. Respite care can also assist the individual by giving diversity, stimulation, and a welcome break from routine.

• Rehabilitation Care

Rehabilitation Care is temporary, specialized care to help patients regain strength, mobility, and function after an injury, illness, or other life-altering event, such as a stroke or fall. Possible therapies include physical, occupational, and speech.

Advantages of Senior-Living Communities

1. Promotes a Low-Maintenance Lifestyle

Retirement communities take care of house maintenance responsibilities, from raking leaves to washing clothes. Furthermore, the senior home provides a secure environment where people might explore new hobbies.

Amenities and communal places in retirement communities vary but may include:

- Tennis courts
- Walking pathways, outdoor gardens, or courtyards
- Theater spaces
- Business centers
- Darts and billiards
- Patios with fireplaces and kitchens
- Spas, jacuzzies, and massage rooms
- Salons or barber shops
- Lending libraries
- Happy hours with cocktails and snacks
- Bingo or board game nights.
- Outings to local cultural centers and events
- Restaurant-style dining programs

2. Encourages Healthy Senior Living

Fitness is crucial to a senior's well-being, from chair yoga to Zumba and strength training.

Some examples of fitness programs and outdoor activities that are available in some senior communities.

- Fitness equipment, scheduled exercise classes
- Golf excursions

- Yoga lessons
- Walking groups
- Group exercise courses
- Fitness centers and free weights
- Hikes and greenways in the area
- Swimming pools (perhaps both indoor and outdoor), swimming and water aerobics

Residents with limited mobility or significant health problems can receive help from the staff.

3. Ensures Safety and Security

Retirement communities have alert systems in each apartment house to promote safety and peace of mind.

4. Provides Personal Care Services

You can have many daily chores done for you, such as housekeeping and lawn care. Then you can focus on what you'd rather do, living life to the fullest.

5. Offers transportation services.

Dependable transportation is provided to nearby shopping malls, restaurants, activities, and doctor's appointments. You may keep a car or maybe give up all the bother of maintaining a vehicle.

6. Emphases Nutrition

Tired of the hassles of cooking, grocery shopping, and dishwashing? Residents in senior communities enjoy tasty food that meets their nutritional needs and a variety of meal options provided by culinary specialists. In addition, restaurant-style dining rooms encourage residents to share meals with friends and family, making each gathering a fun social occasion.

7. Encourages socialization

Socialization is a primary reason many people live in a senior living community, which can provide you with an active social life. To meet peers in your community, you can join a music group, a games club, or a new fitness class. Active citizens enjoy activity calendars that are packed with fun and engaging learning opportunities, such as:

- Travel clubs
- Book clubs
- Coffee get-togethers
- Bingo or board game nights
- Spiritual/religious study circles
- Clubs for playing cards and Mahjong
- Advisory boards for the community
- Morning brunches and evening happy hours

How to look for a senior community:

There are several elements to consider when looking for the perfect senior living community.

The Senior Living Guidebook has a list of every community available near you. The consumer data from the guide can be sorted by service type, cost, or zip code, and provides additional resources for researching senior living communities in your area. The Senior Living Guidebook is available on their website or mobile application. You can also find senior living sites at "A Place for Mom": www.aplaceformom.com/best-of-senior-living-award

Of course, you'll want to visit the community. Talk to residents, if possible.

Questions to ask when interviewing a Senior Living Community

- Does the community provide memory care when needed?

- Does the facility have human service professionals who can check on residents and provide assistance throughout the day?

- Do residents choose their meals?

- Is there a nearby shopping mall? Are any of the following "musts" or priorities?

- Is the community pet-friendly?

- Is it close to familiar doctors or places of worship?

- Are there flexible mealtimes?

- Can guests and relatives spend the night?

Also, checking out reviews and testimonials on websites like Senior Housing Providers can give you a general idea of how the community will be when you're there. Retired people should be able to spend most of their time doing what they want.

If you're planning to relocate, spend time in your new location before you decide.

My preferred living arrangement would be _____

>13 <
Financial Management

"The way to avoid running out of money in retirement is: a) have a lot of it. b) spend it very carefully."

"It's good to have money and the things that money can buy, but it's good, too, to check up once in a while and make sure that you haven't lost the things that money can't buy."
    —George Lorimer.

"Money is a terrible Master but an excellent Servant."
    -P.T. Barnum

As Spock on Star Trek said, "Live long and prosper."

Seriously, this chapter was written by a finance professional, and it will help you with this issue that likely is on your mind.

Your financial well-being is an important aspect at this stage.

This chapter addresses the important components of your financial situation and touches on some legal aspects of your life going forward. It's recognized that everyone is different, but there are common considerations.

"Longevity risk—the risk of running out of assets before you run out of time— is one of the things retirees fear most," says Wade D. Pfau, co-director of the American College of Financial Services Center for Retirement Income. "A long life is a great outcome, but it brings a large financial burden."

For many, traditional pensions also can provide lifetime income, although usually without inflation protection.

However, outside of government employment, pensions are largely disappearing.

The longevity challenge is most important for higher-income workers who'll depend on their investments for their retirement income. It's critical to have a firm handle on how long those investments must last to sustain them.

Here's some of the nitty-gritty of Social Security:

- The Social Security program is designed to provide automatic longevity protection — life benefits indexed to inflation. Social Security will replace a larger share of lower-income workers' employment income than that of higher-income workers.

- If you can afford to defer claiming Social Security to as late as 70, you may get greater lifetime benefits by living long enough. (The break-even age is usually between 80 and 85, when larger monthly checks make up for preceding benefits by deferring to age 70)

- A surviving spouse can collect 100% of the late spouse's benefit if the survivor has reached full retirement age 66 (as of 2022), but the amount will be lower if the deceased spouse claimed benefits before he or she reached full retirement age. If you receive Social Security benefits on your OWN work history, this will affect the amount you can receive as a surviving spouse. Full retirement age is dependent on your birth year. The FRA is 66 years and two months for those born in 1955, increasing gradually to 67 for those born in 1960 or later.

Are you going to outlive your money? A rule of thumb is that you'll need 10 times your income at retirement.

4% Rule

How to decide how much you can/should withdraw from your retirement funds each year? The 4% Rule is a practical rule of thumb you can use. The point is to keep a steady income stream while maintaining an adequate overall account balance for future years. Withdrawals will be primarily from interest and dividends on savings. Some experts say the 4% withdrawal rate is the best option. Other knowledgeable financial advisors say that 5% is better for all but the worst-case scenarios and some believe that 3% may be safer in current conditions regarding interest rates. Your financial advisor can be very helpful in assisting you to decide.

Retirement calculator

This tool can help you calculate how much you will need in retirement with a personalized snapshot based on your desired lifestyle.

https://www.aarp.org/membership/benefits/finance/retirement-calculator/

You will enter data such as marital status, age, savings, Social Security benefits, and lifestyle preference. This last category has three general levels:

Spend Less: for example: eat at home more, travel less often to fewer locations or shorter distances, use fewer utilities, buy fewer new clothes, etc.

Spend the Same: you expect to continue spending similarly to now.

Spend More: eat at restaurants more often, buy more gifts for family/friends, take more vacations or travel farther for longer periods, etc.

Using cash instead of a card where possible (such as grocery shopping, department stores, restaurants, coffee shops, nights out, etc.) makes spending much more tangible.

Keeping score of your financial status

Income is a flow concept, and wealth is a static concept. Your Social Security check is a flow concept, and the value of your home minus the mortgage is a wealth concept. You pay your bills from flows; sometime in the future, your wealth may be converted to income flows such as selling your home.

The first thing to do is create a balance sheet (sometimes called a net worth statement). Knowing your current status is important so you have a starting point. You need a way to keep score, and this is the accepted way of doing so.

On a piece of paper or a spreadsheet, create two columns. On the right are items you own (house, car, other assets), and in a column on the left list your debts. At the bottom, subtract your debts from your assets; this is your net worth.

Spending   What level of living do you want? What standard of living is acceptable? The most important challenge is spending less than your income. This is simple in theory but not always possible. See below for creating a budget or, better said, a list of necessary expenses and a list of income. Seeing the reality of your situation is useful.

It is interesting to note that many wealthy people do not buy fancy cars, nor do they live in mansions.

Debt

Except for a mortgage, avoid debt. Credit card debt is the most serious. The interest rate is high, and sometimes purchases are made without a person's capacity to cover the cost, at least at the time of purchase. Credit cards are very useful, but only if funds are available to pay off that debt before the end of the cycle requiring payment. Paying on time will also elevate your credit rating. If there is credit card debt, don't buy anything that can't be paid in full at the end of the next cycle. Make a plan to pay off the debt as soon as possible. Save up for a large purchase.

<u>Do not</u> co-sign loans for your grandchildren - college loans, car loans, or home loans. You are at risk for 100% of the loan, and they may default on the loan or assume it is a gift. Furthermore, it could put your relationship at risk. So seriously, <u>just</u> <u>don't</u> <u>do</u> <u>it</u>. If you want to give them something, make it an outright gift.

Create a budget.

Will my money last? This is the central question. Make sure you put aside <u>more</u> than you think you need.

Put together a budget. Separate your budget into absolute needs and your wants (less-than-absolutely necessary). Once done, compare your income with your budget. If you're handy with a spreadsheet, create one; otherwise, make one on paper. Create 12 rows of months, showing your expenses in one column and in the next column your income. This can be very illuminating to show the direction of your financial well-being. Be sure to allow for irregular or unplanned expenses such as your water heater failing, your car dying, or your roof needing replacement.

If you have $48K annually, that means $4000 per month. How does that compare to your budget? If $2,000 comes from Social Security, the other $2,000 comes from your saved resources or investments. Emergency funds, or "Rainy Day" accounts, should be $10-12K annually. That would leave $36K or $3,000 monthly.

Try out your level of spending <u>before</u> retirement if you can. Adjust as needed to find where you're comfortable.

If you're not at that point of a balanced spending level, consider potential sources of income. Uncomfortable as it may be, going back to work full-time or part-time may be an option. Consider all options; you may have skills and interests that fit well into full or part-time work. It doesn't have to be forever, but it's a good option if one's health and energy level allow it. We all need a reason to start the day, and if spending some time earning additional income is useful, consider doing something useful for yourself and others.

Empower.com is a free online grid of your financial situation, including net worth, asset allocation, and a retirement calculator.

Many Americans worry they're not saving enough for retirement, and rightfully so.

Almost 40 million households have no retirement savings [National Institute on Retirement Security].

Americans have a retirement savings deficit of $3.68 trillion. [estimate from Employee Benefit Research Institute]

About 71% of U.S. adults admit that their financial planning needs improvement. However, only 29% of Americans work with a financial advisor. [2020 Northwestern Mutual study]

The value of working with a financial advisor can vary by person. Advisors are legally prohibited from promising returns, but research suggests that people who work with a financial advisor feel more at ease about their finances. They could have about 15% more money to spend in retirement.

On average, a hypothetical $500K investment would grow to over $3.4 million under the care of an advisor over 25 years. Compare this to the expected self-management value of $1.69 million, or 50% less. In other words, over 25 years, an advisor-managed portfolio would average 8% annualized growth, compared to 5% from a self-managed portfolio. [A recent Vanguard study]

Brighter news: Many Americans are saving for retirement.

Fidelity reported that the total 401(k) savings rate for the first quarter of 2022 reached 14%. The total Fidelity IRA accounts increased by 11% over the first quarter of 2021. The average 401(k) balance for those saving for over 10 years averaged over $380,000.

General guidelines for retirement savings

You should aim 3 times a year's salary by age 40, 6x by 50, and 8x by 60, hoping to save 10x when it's time to retire. [Fidelity research].

These recommendations are based on a target retirement age of 67 and a person saving 15% of their income at age 25 and investing at least 50% in stocks. Saving for retirement is different for everyone. If you feel like you're behind in savings, want to make sure you're on track, or want to find investment vehicles to help you save more, talking to an advisor can help you set and execute a retirement plan.

Each advisor has a unique strategy. Some advisors may suggest aggressive investments, while others are more conservative. If you prefer to go all in on stocks, an advisor that prefers bonds and index funds is not a great match for your style. However, a skilled advisor can adjust to your preferences.

American's Average Retirement Savings by Age

An October 2020 study by the Center for Retirement Research calculated median retirement account (401(k)/IRA) balances by age from Federal Reserve survey data. Here are the numbers:

- 35 to 44: $51,000
- 45 to 54: $90,000
- 55 to 64: $120,000

A financial advisor can help you feel more at ease about your finances, and you could end up with about 15% more money for retirement spending.

See the section on Selecting an Advisor with whom to work.

Time related to financial well-being

Time is both our friend and enemy. We must accept that time changes our environment and perception of time. The hard part is accepting that change is not negotiable, accepting what is happening, and making adjustments that fit as closely as possible to your goals.

See the section about Portfolio Income under Sources of Income

Economic environment

History suggests that the Federal Reserve System is not particularly adept or wise. The system was created so as not to be subjected to political forces, but evidence suggests this is false. In this writing, the Fed influences the forces of inflation and is trying to remedy the increase. No one knows the outcome. In any case, one can reasonably surmise that political forces will influence Fed policy, be this interest rate changes and/or quantitative easing as we move along over time. We are left to our own devices to manage our affairs, but there's no shortage of people willing to share their opinions.

Managing Risk

Risk addresses the unknown outcomes and events that threaten your situation. We can assess the risk to determine if we wish to transfer the risk elsewhere. The "elsewhere" are insurance companies in return for paying a premium. Here are some common risks you may face.

Insurance considerations

Do you need <u>long-term care</u>? Many people will need it but some will not.

According to the Dept. of Health and Human Services, 70% of people who reach the age of 65 will need long-term care, whether provided by families or by paid caregivers/nursing homes. aspe.hhs.gov/reports/what-lifetime-risk-needing-receiving-long-term-services-supports

You don't know which side of this statistic you will be on; however, there are long-term care policies that cover the occurrence. They are expensive, but so is long-term care. The younger a person is, the less expensive these policies are. An alternative is a hybrid life insurance policy that pays the death benefit towards long-term care, if necessary, but it does reduce the death benefit. They are somewhat less expensive. It's worth the effort to shop around.

<u>Death</u> If someone depends on you for income and your death occurs prematurely, life insurance may be the answer. Sometimes, a life insurance policy is purchased to provide an inheritance to children or others. Normally, but not always, a term policy is preferred. Personal situations and desires drive the choice.

Accidents   We are all at risk from various activities. Using good judgment about one's activities is important. Do you need to clean the gutters? Or blow the leaves off your roof? Falling is often a risk. For this reason, as you age, you should practice balance improvement.

Health insurance is vital. At 65, Medicare is available but apply before your 65th birthday. However, Medicare is not adequate. Consider a supplemental policy. There are many choices, but consider an Advantage Plan, and there are many with zero premiums.

Auto Insurance- The major item in auto insurance is liability protection. Consider your assets and your ability to manage a car. Your financial well-being may suffer if there is a judgment against you after an accident. Each state has minimum liability coverage; the minimum may be adequate. If your auto is a few years old, excluding collision may be worthwhile.

Insurance is expensive, but if your auto is relatively new, selecting a policy with a high deductible is often worthwhile. Other items, such as comprehensive and medical coverage, may be desirable but unnecessary. Having coverage for repairs while on the road may be important. Changing a flat tire or having gasoline delivered to you may be worthwhile. Normally, new cars have fewer problems on the road. Be sure to shop around for auto insurance. Each company competes with others, so rates are always changing. Having a good driving record reduces the premium.

Homeowners/renters insurance. Owning a home or renting a living space comes with potential liabilities. Even a small fire can be a large loss but having a guest or someone else at your residence suffer a mishap can result in a lawsuit. Most mortgage companies require some kind of coverage. Consider your circumstances as to the value of your personal belongings and the possibility of someone in your residence suffering an accident.

Umbrella Insurance. This insurance provides coverage above that provided by your auto and homeowners/rental liability limits. Normally, one million dollars is the most common coverage, and it's not expensive but also depends on your net worth, lifestyle, and sense of risk aversion.

Medicare and Medicaid - Several months before your 65th birthday, apply for Medicare. This is a valuable asset to your health insurance coverage; however, you need supplemental coverage as Medicare doesn't cover everything. Many private insurers offer Medicare Supplement coverage. Do some investigation; it's easy online. Consider an Advantage Plan carefully; most, not all, have zero premiums. Still, you must pay a minimum to meet with a specialist but are zero with your primary care provider. Laboratory work and x-rays sometimes have a fee. Plan D can cover some prescription costs.

Medicaid is available for low-income, low-wealth persons; qualification is complex. An elder care attorney would normally be involved.

If you feel you may qualify for Social Security Disability, consult with an elder law attorney. It is a difficult process; this attorney could help you. It may take two or three attempts to be successful.

How retirees and retirement savers should prepare for a recession

There have been 11 recessions since 1948, and a recession may or may not happen in 2023. But as the ants prepared for winter, and the grasshopper just fiddled away, not thinking about what he might face when winter comes, you can take some steps to prepare for "what if ...."

1. **Save**. Avoid risk if you think a recession is around the corner," says John Lonski, president of Thru the Cycle, an investment advisory firm. Financial planners often recommend that you have six months' worth of expenses in your emergency fund. With the Federal Reserve raising rates, money market mutual funds' interest rates are very competitive.

2. **Save for extras**. Rather than using credit for an item in your "want" category, put aside money for it and buy it when that piggy bank has enough.

3. **Pay down debt**. The money you save in interest can be used to build your emergency fund. And, all things being equal, paying off a credit card that charges 16 percent interest is the same as earning 16 percent on your money.

4. **Keep a cash stash**. Retirees taking withdrawals from their savings should keep about a year's worth of expenses in cash in their retirement account. Bear markets in stocks typically last about a year. You don't want to sell stocks when the market falls unless there's no other option. If your investments are down 10 percent and you withdraw 5 percent, your account is down 15 percent.

5. **Stay safe**. Most cash options pay little-to-nothing in interest. Money market mutual funds, a typical cash

option in brokerage accounts, currently pay 4.5 percent interest. However, it's better than a 20 to 30 percent loss from stocks in a bear market. Taking cash withdrawals from the money-market portion of your retirement account during a bear market gives your other, riskier investments time to recover.

6. **Stay on the sidelines**. Sooner or later, you'll be tempted to buy stocks that appear cheap. Take your time going back in. Keep in mind that by the time the National Bureau of Economic Research (NBER) has officially declared a recession has started, it's probably near the end. After all, economic data usually lags particularly GDP. The average recession lasts about 10 months, and the NBER typically needs about nine months to collect all the data it needs to declare that a recession has started. If you wish to reenter the market, consider dollar-cost-averaging. This means adding a small amount to your portfolio each month.

Where to live?

Most people who live in a single-family residence desire to remain there. However, for good reasons, living in a retirement situation may be advantageous-- an apartment, a retirement village, or a continuing-care facility. Moving in with the next generation may also be possible.

Senior living options are considered in Chapter 12.

Income sources

The foundation of household income is Social Security. When to begin? For most eligible participants, age 62 is the earliest age to start. The benefits max out at age 70. When to start receiving benefits is a complicated and uncertain exercise because we don't know when we will die, and there are no benefits to non-spouses at death. [Note: Unmarried children under age 18 can be eligible to receive Social Security survivors' benefits.] Income cash flow is important here. If has a family history of longevity, and is in good health, waiting to age 70 may be beneficial, when possible. While waiting, each year, benefits increase by about 8%. A good financial advisor should have the appropriate software to help with this decision.

If not yet done, register with the Social Security Administration at: **www.ssa.gov**. There's much information on this site that shows your benefits at various ages.

<u>Pension</u> Over time, pensions have become less popular in the private sector but remain in the public sector. A pension is a great addition to household income. Normally, payments start at retirement, and inflation adjustments are not common. Do consult an advisor, as important decisions must be made at retirement.

Supplementing income with a job

A bit of paid work

Whether full-time or part-time, working to supplement household income should be considered. There are many benefits beyond the salary, such as socialization and benefits.

Finding a job

- Best jobs for seniors over 60 from Indeed.com: Part-Time Jobs for Seniors Over 60
 https://www.indeed.com/career-advice/finding-a-job/best-jobs-for-seniors-over-60
- from glassdoor.com
 https://www.glassdoor.com/blog/guide/best-jobs-for-seniors-over-60/

- High-Paying Online Jobs for People Over 50
  https://www.youtube.com/watch?v=FuN5F-iN5Es
- Make Money, Stay Active, and Thrive at Work as a Senior
  https://www.greatseniorliving.com/articles/jobs-for-older-people
- Seniors at Work: A growing trend
  https://www.greatseniorliving.com/articles/jobs-for-older-people#growing-trend
- 31 good jobs for older people based on different motivations
  https://www.greatseniorliving.com/articles/jobs-for-older-people#different-motivations.
- 8 benefits of working as a senior
  https://www.greatseniorliving.com/articles/jobs-for-older-people#benefits
- Age Discrimination and your job search
  https://www.greatseniorliving.com/articles/jobs-for-older-people#age-discrimination
- Looking for jobs as an older person: Practical tips
  https://www.greatseniorliving.com/articles/jobs-for-older-people#practical-tips

There are companies that pay you for being online. You can do tasks like reading emails, taking surveys, playing games, and watching videos or even TV. InboxDollars has paid over $59 million in cash rewards to its members since it started in the 2000s. That comes down to $8,194 being paid out to members every day just for being online!

The brands and partners pay InboxDollars for consumer input from members like you. The information you provide helps influence future products and services, in addition to earning you some free cash. Once you join, you can complete any online activity you choose – There may be paid surveys, paid videos and tv to watch; perhaps you will be redeeming grocery coupons, free food, and more. By completing these, you get real cash rewards, not points! An additional perk is that members may also enjoy promos and contests to win money online, get free printable coupons, beauty samples and other free stuff online.   https://www.inboxdollars.com/

Annuity

There's a huge difference of opinion on the usefulness of annuities. Annuities are a tool; sometimes they fit, and sometimes do not. They are complicated, and salespeople tend to emphasize positive attributes. Agents selling annuities may be more interested in sales-- from which their income is derived-- than in what is the best benefit to you. Personal circumstances inform the decision. A fee-only advisor can guide you based on your situation and would not be influenced by commission profit.

For charitable annuities, see Chapter 15 (Legacy)

Reverse Mortgage

This means augmenting household income by selling your house while living there. This results in your not having to make mortgage payments. An offer is made to you, usually by a bank, for the monthly payment, which extends to your life. At death, the buyer assumes ownership of the house. A fee-only advisor must evaluate the terms of the offer competently in light of the household income requirements.

Portfolio income

The dream is investing in the stock market and making a lot of money. It's a good dream, and over time, it will work. However, with fewer years available, a different strategy is called for. For shorter lengths of time, holding growth stocks has many risks. An alternative is holding solid dividend-paying stocks, hopefully with a history of increasing the dividends over time. Selecting these stocks is not easy as there are many variables to consider. One can do this independently, but it takes time, effort, knowledge, and software to analyze the portfolio. However, a dividend-paying portfolio reduces portfolio risk and provides income.

Leave stocks as they are, for the most part. At an average 6% annual gain in the market, you will double your investment in 12 years.

A good portfolio manager can provide information on your portfolio of investments, when to use Money Market, and when to buy or sell stocks or bonds, but the advisor selection is important. More on this topic later.

Qualified Plan withdrawals

One may begin withdrawals from a qualified plan at age 59½, but there are rules, whether from a 401(k), a 403(b) or a 457. The tax basis of the assets in a qualified plan is zero, meaning that withdrawals are taxed as ordinary income. This might or may not be significant, but starting at age 70, withdrawals must begin. The government wants its share of what you have saved. One option to escape the tax bite is to move the Required Minimum Distribution (RMD) amount to a 501(c) organization. This means the money is donated, but the tax is eliminated. This is an excellent strategy if one can afford the transfer and is a philanthropist.

Become a landlord.

Becoming a landlord is becoming an entrepreneur. You are investing capital (perhaps borrowed) with the expectation of a return, but with an understanding there is risk involved. The fundamental question to address is cash flow. Does the monthly revenue cover the costs of owning and managing the property? Managing the property has costs – the landlord may assume the property management costs or outsource it to a management company.

There are also property taxes, property, and liability insurance premiums, etc., to consider. Therefore, the monthly rental income should more than cover these expenses. Is a gain certain? That must be carefully considered. It is important to avoid negative cash flow. The cash flow analysis is very important – perhaps a spreadsheet project is appropriate with some adjustment for uncertainty.

The decision quality at the outset is critical as it likely affects the outcome. Many people have made good landlord decisions and done well, but some have not.

Family

Family members can perhaps be called upon to help with household income. This is not an easy solution, often with pride involved, but perhaps necessary. Sometimes, a small monthly transfer can help with expenses to maintain the standard of living you wish. A candid discussion with offspring may avoid an embarrassing situation.

Financial Documents

Everyone needs a will plus some other documents. They won't remember you fondly if you don't take this step. Your survivors want to know your wishes – the purpose of estate documents. A will is the first step. After that, a *financial power of attorney* and then a *health-care power of attorney*. You do not want to die intestate. Your state already has an estate plan for you unless you indicate otherwise. Likely, you would not approve or like the intestate plan, so take charge and make your wishes known. A Living Will is particularly useful if someone has to make medical decisions on your behalf when you can't-- when to let go, what measures should be taken to prolong life, etc. These are tough decisions, but here you can make your wishes known. It's a great comfort to those you care about so they know what to do.

An additional step but not a legal step and not required is to write a personal letter that outlines your wishes regarding the distribution of personal effects, last rites, etc. This document is legally nonbinding but very helpful to your heirs.

Do you need an attorney? Maybe or maybe not.

Wills

Having your estate documents is very important.

For simple estates, it's feasible to do it yourself. There's an online product called WillMaker, distributed by Intuit, which is very good and is valid in all states. WillMaker will likely suffice if your estate is relatively simple, you do not need a trust, and it's easy to use and valid.

Go to www.willmaker.com. There is a small cost, but it's legal in your state of residence. One simply answers questions; the software creates your documents. It can create several important documents. Recommended are a will, power of attorney for financial affairs, health care power of attorney, and a living will.

You may use www.legalzoom.com Legalzoom.com is a resource for working out a do-it-yourself will, living trust, and estate-plan document. Use an attorney's services if your situation requires a trust.

A <u>Do-it-Yourself Will</u> is one you write yourself instead of having an estate attorney write it for you. Several free online forms can be found using the sites mentioned in the resources in Appendix 2.

In addition to legalzoom.com, there are:
- eforms.com/wills/ includes Last Will and Testaments (Wills): By State; What to Include in a Will; Sample; How

to Make a Will; How to Sign a Will; How to Amend a Will; Frequently Asked Questions; Estate Planning Checklist

- freewill.com
- legalcontracts.com
- doityourselfdocuments.com

Living trust

This differs from a will in that it bypasses the probate process. A trustee is designated to carry out explicit directions for the distribution of assets after the death of the person creating the living trust. Living trusts can be either revocable (the person creating it has the power to change trust rules at any time) or irrevocable, which differ in tax treatment and flexibility. Assets that can be assigned to the trust include real estate, financial accounts, personal property (such as art, antiques, and jewelry), and business interests. Establishing a living trust usually requires an attorney.

Contact an estate lawyer for more complex situations in wills and living trusts.

Estate plan – An estate planning checklist guides how to plan an individual's assets and end-of-life health care if they should become incapacitated or die. You can decide who you would like to handle personal finances if you should not be able to yourself. In addition, you can establish who will get what after your death.

Planning forms are available online.

https://www.legalcontracts.com/contracts/groups/

Click on Family & Estate

You'll start with an inventory of assets. The tangible assets in an estate may include:

Homes, land, or other real estate; vehicles including cars, motorcycles, or boats; Collectibles such as coins, art, antiques, or trading cards; other personal possessions. The intangible assets in an estate may include checking and savings accounts and certificates of deposit; stocks, bonds, and mutual funds; life insurance policies; retirement plans such as workplace 401(k) plans and individual retirement accounts; health savings accounts; ownership in a business. The document should include any liabilities (debts, etc.)

Passing on your Wealth

Probate is distributing one's estate to one's choice of heirs. This is normally done via a well-written will, and assets can be distributed to heirs as the normal process of the probate process.

However, there may exist circumstances where the assets are not to be distributed lump-sum but perhaps over time or subject to conditions; for this, a trust may be required. The trust can be created within the will (testamentary trust), which comes into being at death. A trustee is selected along with the trust beneficiaries, plus the conditions specified for the trustee to follow. For example, a minor as the beneficiary requires trust. A person with limited decision-making ability may require trust to manage his/her assets.

You may start the distribution process before death, transferring assets as a gift. An argument for this process is based on superior knowledge of the beneficiary and his/her values/behavior and/or needs. This strategy is done through gifting. Each year, the amount of the gift to any one person is approximately $17,000 without any tax effect but adjusted annually by the rate of inflation.

Should the reader be blessed with a particularly large estate, there are sophisticated strategies to transfer assets to the next generation with minimal estate tax.

Variations on this theme driven by individual circumstances can be analyzed and handled by attorneys and financial advisors.

Taxes

For many households, federal and state taxes are significant. Many people feel that there's some secret strategy to avoid these taxes, but unhappily Congress and the IRS have structured the tax code to make it very difficult to avoid/reduce income taxes. The truth is that employed persons, those who receive a W-9 statement each January, have few opportunities to reduce current taxation. This is done by design. Nevertheless, employee taxation deferral is possible via 401K, Roth 401K, and 457. If the employer does not offer a retirement program, an IRA contribution is available if household cash flow will support it.

However, if self-employed income is coming into the household, a simplified employee retirement program is possible: an IRA or a Roth 401K. A Roth solo 401(k) is a retirement plan that allows contributions by a business owner and their spouse who is involved in the business.

As a parallel strategy, starting a home business may be useful for tax purposes. For example, if an auto is needed, it can be owned by the business, so all expenses from auto use may be deductible, including depreciation. Expenses such as internet and phone plus a dedicated office space in the home may be deductible. This requires a Schedule C to be filed, which may increase tax compliance expenses. This is a rational choice but requires analysis beyond the scope of this book.

Many of your considerations covered in this chapter can be made clearer and easier with the aid of a financial advisor. "Do I need one?", Aren't they an expense that taps into my resources? you may ask. "I'm not wealthy." This is even more reason to engage one to analyze your financial situation. He/she can assist you in protecting the wealth you do have.

Selecting an advisor with whom to work

"Before you invest, investigate." Much has been written and promoted about using an advisor, and while personality is important, there are professional considerations.

First, consider the advisor's technical knowledge and that he/she uses new software that enables the advisor to analyze households, the market, the economy, etc. This technology constantly changes, and advisors must stay abreast of current developments.

Second, evaluate the advisor's experience; one with years of experience can bring wisdom.

Third, one of the most valuable attributes of an advisor is objectivity. To say it in another way, an advisor is not you, so he is not burdened by your situation with all its emotional content. Listen carefully. The recommendations may not be what you expected, but they may be valuable.

Fourth, is the advisor a Registered Investment Advisor? RIA stands for Registered Investment Advisor and can be federal or state; that doesn't matter. Further, an RIA is subject to either federal or state oversight. Having the designation RIA means he/she is a fiduciary. A fiduciary is required to place your interest above her/his own. Interview several and request their ADV, a document they must provide their clients. It is a full-disclosure document. Study it closely. If none is provided, move on. This is a document of total disclosure. If one is not forthcoming, move on.

How much does the advice cost? The most common is a fee by the hour or based on assets under management. Sometimes an annual fee for all services rendered is used. Recall that whatever the cost, it must be fair to both parties. Commissions, if any, must be minimal. An advisor is in business, and his/her services are not free. An advisor charging fees is much better than one who earns commissions.

Fifth, another item that is important in selecting an advisor but sometimes overlooked is: Does the advisor have adequate academic training to do the job? An undergraduate degree in economics, accounting, or finance is minimal.

In addition, being a Certified Financial Planner is important. This is like having a master's degree. The training is broad and specific to the practice, and it suggests a commitment to it. A Certified Financial Planner has agreed to a set of practice standards that are rigorous and includes total confidentiality.

Finally, is communication positive and useful? Are you being heard and/or understood? Does the advisor listen? There must be a substantial interchange level, so everyone understands the circumstances involved. You must feel comfortable with your choice. Will the advisor respond to phone or email questions within a short period?

Trust is critical and very difficult to determine and judge. Trust has likely been established if the advisor has been practicing for many years. However, interviewing current clients is useful. Do not be bashful – ask the hard questions. Does the advisor respond to inquiries? Are inquiries welcome? What level of communication can you expect? Do you like the advisor? Do you feel comfortable with difficult topics?

Given that, interview several advisors; the answer will come to you as to which advisor will be in your best interest.

It's common to think of an advisor as a money manager. Yes, that is one function, but high-quality decision-making is a more important function. A good advisor will guide you in any decision-making process. Whether it's to buy a car, change residence, retire, or change the structure of your estate documents. A good financial advisor will be comfortable in all these areas and guide you not to make the decisions but to consider all the factors involved. This is an argument for comprehensive financial and estate planning. Good advisors are comfortable and practiced in doing so.

Understanding these terms and their relevance to your situation will add to your comfort and skill in managing your financial situation.

Tax-Deferred Retirement Plans

The plans referred to here and popular are Qualified Plans. This means the funds in these plans are tax-deferred except for a special class called Roth Plans. There are many such tax-deferred plans: 401(k), 403(b) 457, SEP, and Simple IRAs and IRAs. Funds must come from earned income, and tax is deferred until withdrawn. There are many rules governing these plans. One of the most popular is the 401(k). These are employer-sponsored, as are the 403(b) and 457. Simplified Employee Plans (SEP) and Simple IRAs are employer-sponsored but are designed for small businesses.

IRAs are well-known and popular. While IRAs are simple on the surface, they also have many rules. Each year, the government announces the maximum amount that can be contributed, which is adjusted by the inflation rate. A higher amount can be contributed if the contributor is 50 or older.

Roth IRAs and 401(k)s are unique because after-tax dollars are contributed, the tax liability is forever gone, and Required Minimum Distributions (RMD) are also gone. The choice between using a Roth plan or a regular one mostly depends on one's situation and expected situation. Here is a case where a tax preparer or an advisor can help.

RMDs are required beginning at age 73. The annual amount is calculated based on the age and value of the account(s) on the last business day of the previous year. The amount distributed is taxed as ordinary income. In some households, some annual philanthropic giving is done. All or a portion of the RMD can be donated, wiping out the tax liability.

Tax-deferred plans can be a significant contributor to retirement wealth. There are projection models which show the feasibility of using these plans. Advisors have these models, but some are available online.

Before age 72, withdraw a bit each year from before-tax IRAs. Part or all of the distribution can be rolled into a Roth IRA.

Smart tips that you may already be following:

Have only one or two credit cards and pay off outstanding balances each month.

Collect and pay bills twice a month only. You can choose when to pay them off and, if possible, do it online. Monitor your credit card statement each month.

Recurring bills can be set up as automatic payments.

If friends or relatives don't like accumulating possessions, give consumable or experiential (spa, tickets, gift cards) gifts.

You should familiarize yourself with the financial issues covered in this chapter. They will help you control your financial situation, which is vital in these years after retirement.

"Money is only a tool. It will take you wherever you wish but will not replace you as the driver." --Ayn Rand

An idea from this chapter I intend to use is:

_____

> 14 <
Senior Citizens' Discounts & Benefits

"The great thing about getting older is that you don't lose all the other ages you've been."—Madeleine L'Engle

"You can't help getting older, but you don't have to get old."--
George Burns

One way to enjoy a more rewarding life after retirement is to explore ways to take advantage of senior discounts or service and health care benefits.

AARP offers an online Safe Driving course that can mean a discount on your automobile insurance.

Many businesses now recognize the value of senior citizen customers and offer discounts and benefits to attract them.

Offering discounted or free services that promote seniors' health and wellness, such as gym memberships or community exercise classes, and senior citizen discounts and benefits can be a great way for businesses to attract customers and show appreciation for older adults.

Senior discounts can save you substantial money — 10% to 80% off the normal price of a wide range of goods and services, including restaurant meals, travel, and even prescription drugs.

You can take advantage of many senior discounts when you are as young as 50. Many senior discounts require you to have a membership or show proof of age. You can ask a business if it offers discounts and whether you qualify for one.

The age for senior discounts ranges from 50 to 65, with most deals starting at age 55 or 60. For the earliest deals, you'll want to join the AARP, which is required for quite a few senior discounts.

Membership in the AARP costs $16 per year, with discounts for paying for multiple years in advance or signing up for an automatically renewing membership. You can join at any age, but full benefits kick off at age 50 — including discounted prices at restaurants, entertainment, travel, and more. It wouldn't take much for the membership to pay for itself.

Expect senior discounts to average around 10% off, though some are as much as 30% off. Some senior discounts are less clear: Many hotel and airfare deals simply offer "discounted rates," which vary in quality.

Sometimes senior deals aren't even the best, so it's important to shop around and check out available discounts. For example, the discounted rates you see for air and hotel aren't necessarily good; sometimes, they are beaten by other discounts available. It pays to double-check and shop around rather than simply expecting the senior discount to be the best way to save.

Health Care - Medicare Advantage Plans. Many health care insurance plans offer low-cost or free copay amounts. Compare providers.

How to get Senior Discounts

Because senior discounts aren't always advertised, you may need to ask. Call ahead or ask in person! You may find deals available from retailers that aren't listed here. You won't know about discounts if you don't ask, which could mean you miss out on great deals.

Most retailers only require you to show your ID (or AARP card) to qualify for senior discount rates. If you're shopping online, you may need to verify age in other ways, such as providing AARP membership information or showing your ID when picking up a product.

Some restaurants may require you to order from a special menu. Some shops offer discounts for seniors on specific days, and you may have to book specific dates for travel to qualify for senior discounts.

Discounts can vary at different locations, particularly at large franchises, where senior discounts are often at the discretion of local management. This is common at restaurants and fast-food locations, where offerings can vary widely between locations. Ask what discounts are available before you buy because the discounts may change.

Senior discounts have been disappearing or have been getting less impressive in recent years. Southwest Airlines, Verizon Wireless, Rite Aid, Kroger, Albertsons, and many more retailers have discontinued or reduced senior discounts, making it even more important for seniors to check for deals and use them when available.

Travel deals are one category where seniors can still find a wide range of great offerings. Seniors can practically always find discounts on hotels and rental cars (up to 30% off) and occasionally special offers for airfare and cruises. Just double-check those rates because we have seen senior fares that aren't the best deal.

Stores with senior discounts (as of 2023):

Dozens of retail stores offer senior discounts — some for people as young as 50. It's a good idea to ask a store manager or cashier if the place where you shop offers a discount.

Offer your ID to prove eligibility because you don't look old enough!

The list is too long to name all retail stores offering senior discounts, but here are some examples from popular stores.

Coded as follows: Store/ Percent discount/ Eligibility (age or membership)/ Availability

Clothing Stores
Banana Republic/10%/50+/any day, participating locations

Belk/15%/50+/1st Tue

Kohl's/15%/55+/Wed

Ross Stores/10%/60+/Tue

TJ Maxx/10%/55+/Tue, participating locations

Grocery Shopping Discounts for Seniors
It appears that grocery stores are phasing out senior discounts in favor of overall savings, according to some groups that follow these trends.

Not every store in the chain may participate in senior discounts. But you should ask your local store if they do, and you can still find discounts at the checkout.

GROCERY STORES - Examples of Senior Discounts at

Kroger/10%/55+/ Tue only, Kroger Plus Card required, participating locations.

Harris Teeter / 5%/55+/ Thu only

Piggly Wiggly/5%/60+/ Wed, participating locations

Albertsons55+ 1st Wed of the month at participating locations

Dining Discounts for Seniors
There are plenty of options, from fast food and casual dining to even more pricey restaurants that offer discounts to seniors. Having an AARP membership will add even more restaurants to your discount list.

RESTAURANTS

Applebee's/10% to 15% /60+ /Any day, participating locations

Arby's/10% and/or free drink with purchase/60+/ Any day

Ben & Jerry's /10%/60 and up/ Any day, participating locations

Bonefish Grill/10%/50+/Any day with an AARP card

Boston Market/Varies by location/Varies by location/ Any day, participating locations.

Burger King/10%/60 +/ Any day, participating locations

Bubba Gump Shrimp Company/10%/50+/Any day with AARP card

Carrabba's Italian Grill/10%/50+/Any day with an AARP card

Chick-fil-A/10%/55+/ Any day, participating locations

Cici's Pizza/Select menu items vary by location/Varies by location/Varies by location

Denny's/15%, special senior menu/50+/Any day with AARP card

El Pollo Loco/10%/60+/Varies by location

Fazoli's/Select items/62+/Must be member of Fazoli's Club 62

Hardee's/<=10%, special discounts beverages/55+/Any day , participating locations

IHOP/10%, the special senior menu includes discounted items/55 +/Must have photo ID

Joe's Crab Shack/10%/50+ //Any day with AARP card

KFC/free sm. drink, 5-10% off food/55+/ Any day, partic. locations

McCormick & Schmick's/10%/50+/Any day with an AARP card

McDonald's/Varies by location/55 +/Varies by location

Outback Steakhouse/10%/50 +/Any day with AARP card

Perkins Restaurant/Senior menu includes discounts/55+/Any day, participating locations

Ponderosa Steakhouse/10%/62+/participating locations require proof of age

Popeye's Louisiana Kitchen/10% or free sm drink/55+//Any day, participating locations

Taco Bell/5% and free drink/65+/ Any day, participating locations

Wendy's/10% or discounted drink/55+/ Any day, participating locations

Whataburger Free/ drink with meal purchase/55+/Any day, participating locations

White Castle/10%/62+/ Any day, participating locations

Other sources of discount information for seniors

You can ask for a weekly newsletter from seniordiscountsclub.com.

Online lists of businesses offering senior discounts

https://www.seniorliving.org/finance/senior-discounts

https://www.forbes.com/health/healthy-aging/senior-discounts

https://www.theseniorlist.com/senior-discounts/

https://www.dealnews.com/features/discounts/senior-discounts/

A savings idea from this chapter I intend to use:

_____

> 15 <
Legacy

There's a T-shirt slogan that reads "I INTEND TO LIVE FOREVER … SO FAR SO GOOD"

Facing the end of life, leaving with dignity and grace:

It is a subject people shy away from, but a wise person considers it and makes helpful plans concerning their demise. You should plan ahead and not resort to careless methods that lack forethought. You must ensure your estate is right after you have retired so that your heirs and loved ones can benefit from the work you have done. This can indeed give you peace of mind.

Take the time to think about your legacy. It should not be a burden but a joyous adventure that allows you to share with others.

Everyone should have a legacy plan in place, including what size asset allocation you should have after they retire. Some people are unaware that if their net worth exceeds $12.92 million, they could be subject to an estate tax on death.

Memoir.

If you haven't already begun one, you might want to explore writing a memoir in the coming years. A memoir is an introspective, profoundly personal tale that focuses on the author's experiences, feelings, recollections, and progress. It may cover topics ranging from childhood memories to significant life events, personal relationships, and travel experiences and chronicle personal growth.

It is a personal history written to share with loved ones and usually concentrates on "the good old days." As you reflect, an honest account of your life is revealed.

A memoir can be a meaningful gift to future generations of family members, especially as they strive to understand their roots. This gift is priceless when delivered from the heart and born of experience. A well-written memoir will inspire, enlighten, and motivate those who read it, especially when they relate to your experiences.

Some of the common themes that a memoir may include are:

- The history of your family
- The lives and legacies of your grandparents, parents, and siblings
- Your timeline that includes the highlights of your life (birth, first love, marriage, children's milestones, grandchildren), the low points (losses), the everyday occurrences you consider milestones (your career history)
- Your values and how they were formed growing up in your family and other significant relationships in your life
- How you have grown from these events that shape you today as a person
- How you have impacted other people around you – including successes and failures
- Career and professional experiences: including successes, failures, and lessons learned.
- Travel and adventure: how these experiences have influenced your outlook on the world
- Your philosophical and spiritual reflections and beliefs and how they have shaped a perspective on life

Perhaps you'd like to make a less formal written record of memories and thoughts to aid recall or to pass on to future generations, possibly illustrated with drawings and photographs. Such a memoir can be an adventure into one's past, a political autobiography, or a creative endeavor reflecting on the joys and challenges of life.

Journal

Consider keeping a journal for those interested in creating light or simple notes of their life experience with photos and drawings. A journal is a personal history that one writes for oneself. It is usually an account of current or recent experiences.

It can include things like what you did on a given day or week, how you felt about specific events, the evolution of your thoughts and impressions, and other things you think are essential to your understanding of life at the time. Even if most journal entries focus on current happenings and thoughts, it's interesting to look back at entries from years earlier to see how our perspectives have changed over time.

Some other ideas for journal entries:

- Earliest childhood memory
- A difficult challenge you overcame
- A place you loved returning to
- What is something you can do that many cannot?
- A regret or embarrassing moment
- What are some delightful special childhood memories such as a best birthday?
- Best book and why?
- Best life lesson(s)
- If you could be granted 3 wishes, what would they be? What about one more?
- Describe an impressive person you love or someone you know.

- What is on your bucket list?
- What are you grateful for?
- Something recent that made you smile
- The most interesting food you've had
- A wonderful experience with parents, siblings, or relative (uncle, aunt, grandparent)
- A favorite toy from childhood
- Best trip you've taken
- Where would you go back to in time?
- Characteristics of a best friend
- Your best qualities
- What changes your mood from pos→neg? neg→pos?
- Personal strengths
- What is your favorite aspect of each season?
- What is the best way to spend a rainy day?
- What would you like to study or take a course in?
- Favorite Halloween costume
- Best winter holiday celebration
- Favorite winter activity
- Favorite sport or what sport/activity do you engage in?
- If you could wave a magic wand, what would you change?
- If you could live your life over, what would you change?
- What was your first job?
- First boyfriend/ girlfriend
- Favorite kind of music?
- What kind of dancing do you like?
- What have you done just for yourself?
- What is your proudest moment?
- Favorite sport, or what sport do you play?
- If you could wave a magic wand, what would you change?
- What would you change if you could live over?
- What was your first job?
- What are your favorite kinds of music?
- What have you done just for yourself?

Over time, you might find old journal entries that inspire you with their simplicity or humor; others will remind you of significant people and events in your life that few others know fully.

A journal can reflect the writing process in a relaxed and creative way, inspiring you to write more often or create more entries. Your efforts encourage others to come forward with their own stories and reflections. Many happy people benefit from the opportunity to share their lives with family members and friends, where they can see how their lives have transformed over time and how they have progressed to new levels of self-awareness, personal growth, learning, evaluation, and review. One of the most important things you can do for yourself is create an enduring record of your life for later generations.

The purpose of many journals is to help others understand and grow by sharing lessons learned through what we do daily.

Your epitaph

If you plan to have a gravestone, what will be the epitaph? What memory would you like to have your family have of you? Can you suggest a motto for your life?

A document to prepare ahead:

Don't take your last wishes to the grave. A funeral planner in PDF format for you to download and fill in is *Before I Go, You Should Know*...available at fcaaz.org/slider-3/before-i-go-you-should-know/ It has more than 30 pages to record everything from your preference for burial or cremation to how to close down your social media accounts and online life.

The planner includes:

Your <u>Funeral Plans</u> (preference for place of service; the form of disposition of the body—cremation or burial. Make arrangements to visit these places now.

Where your important papers are; This should be a fireproof box at home, not a safety-deposit box at a bank, because they can be challenging to access and expensive.

- Who should take care of your pets and how
- Whom to contact when the time comes
- Consumer funeral and burial rights and rules specific to your state
- A survivor's checklist of important but often overlooked tasks when death occurs
- A place to record all the biographical information your family will need for an obituary, funeral, or memorial service

Your <u>Will</u> should remain current and up to date. "What if you die without a will? What about your children and surviving spouse?"

In your will, it's essential to clearly state what you want to be done with your personal property. Will you have a standard funeral, or would you prefer something that reflects who you are and how you like to be remembered?

Preference for <u>body disposition</u>—traditional coffin burial, cremation, and the newer, less expensive, less polluting techniques of water cremation ("aquamation") or alkaline hydrolysis, respectively.

Green burial is simple, natural and personal. It occurs without embalming, without metal or steel caskets, and without concrete vaults. The practice of green burial invites families into participating in the act of burying their loved ones. Check on specific legislation in your state.

Bequests and charitable annuities:

While many different ways exist to create a lasting legacy, the two most common ways are bequests and charitable donations.

A <u>bequest</u> is an outright gift of money or property during one's lifetime. The person who has made the endowment usually names a personal representative to carry out the will and administer the estate. There are several ways to make a charitable donation. The simplest is to leave it to an individual or organization of your choice. If you would like to earmark the grant for a specific purpose, some donors set up a charitable trust, similar to a will in that the assets are transferred upon death. Charitable trusts can also be established during life through a living trust. This arrangement is generally used when you want to avoid probate costs and delays but does not need complete control over how the money is used after your death.

A <u>charitable gift annuity</u> is a way of donating money or property to charity, which entitles you to an income from that donation for your lifetime or longer, depending on the terms of your gift annuity agreement (GAA). You can make charitable gifts by giving outright in cash, real estate, or insurance policies. If you lack trust or will, working with your financial advisor and estate-planning attorney is essential to determine how you want your assets distributed after death.

You designate a gift to a charity, which allows you to receive payments from the charity or financial institution, or both. This is a desirable option for retirees who need regular income. Income from charitable gifts can be received through immediate payments, monthly checks, or a stream of expenses that continue indefinitely.

Some people who want to leave a legacy gift want to know what happens with their donation after they are gone. They want a tax benefit, and they want it now! Cash value life insurance offers them just that.

Memorial tree

Plant a tree in someone's honor on municipal or public land (with permission) and have a plaque created for it. Planting a tree to remember a loved one is a living tribute that will benefit current and future generations. Planting this tree in a national forest can serve as a natural monument and engage participants in nature's long-term plan.

You may like to arrange for a tree seedling to be given out to each guest at your funeral.

When planting a memorial tree, consider the best tree species. You may plant an oak tree to represent their wisdom and power. Another choice might be a Rowan tree (Irish tradition) to symbolize their inspiration and protection. The Rowan tree was thought to protect against witchcraft and enchantment, and today grows as a deciduous tree that fruits red berries in the autumn.

A memorial tree is a peaceful physical reminder. These trees help survivors navigate the healing process. Planting a tree is a lovely way to remember a loved one who has died. It also provides an alternative area to visit to commemorate your loved one. Not only that but if properly cared for, the tree will live for many generations. Planting one ensures that your loved one's legacy will live long after passing.

Checklist: Will - done ☐ still needs doing ☐
   ☐ I have written out my burial preferences.
   ☐ My family knows where to find my important papers and passwords.

Dear Reader,

As you reach the final pages of " Reinventing Your Life After Retirement", we hope you have found this journey into retirement redefined both enlightening and inspiring. The exploration of new ventures, body and brain health, financial well-being, social relationships, technology, purposeful downsizing, and legacy is a testament to the boundless possibilities that await you in this remarkable phase of life.

My mission in writing this book was to challenge the traditional narrative of retirement and ignite a spark within you to embrace life's second act with renewed vigor and purpose. We firmly believe that retirement is not a time to fade into the background but an opportunity to unleash your full potential.

If "Reinventing Your Life After Retirement" has provided you with an empowering journey into retirement, has sparked positive changes in your perspective on retirement, we would be immensely grateful if you could take a moment to share your thoughts in a review. Your words carry the power to inspire other readers and encourage them to embark on their own transformative journeys.

Whether it's a few lines or a detailed account of your experience with the book, your review will be a beacon of hope for those standing at the threshold of retirement. Your reflections could help someone else navigate the uncharted waters of this new chapter in life.

By leaving a review, you become an integral part of our community of like-minded individuals who refuse to let age define their aspirations. And discover that this phase of life is brimming with possibilities for growth and fulfillment.

To leave a review, simply visit the platform where you purchased the book or use the QR code below. Your feedback is invaluable to us, and we eagerly look forward to reading your thoughts.

Thank you for accompanying us on this empowering journey into retirement redefined. May your second act be filled with joy, purpose, and endless possibilities!

With gratitude,

Sallie W. Abbas

  Author of

" Reinventing Your Life After Retirement: ..."

Appendix

Build a Backyard <u>Labyrinth</u>

https://www.instructables.com/Build-a-Backyard-Labyrinth/

In place of rope, it can be marked out with small stones.

Another design for a labyrinth, based on the one in the Cathedral at Chartres, France

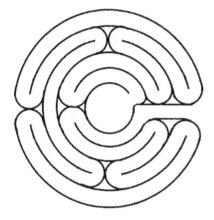

Another website with instructions on building your labyrinth:

https://labyrinthsociety.org/make-a-labyrinth

DIY <u>Little Free Library</u> Plans
Plans for building a neighborhood leave-a-book take-a-book little library can be found at:

www.familyhandyman.com/list/diy-little-free-library-plans/

Burpees
https://www.youtube.com/watch?v=qLBImHhCXSw
https://www.youtube.com/watch?v=tJrdJBWBu08

Yoga for men
bodybyyoga.training/yoga-for-men/yoga-for-men-over-50/

Yoga for older adults
www.forbes.com/health/healthy-aging/best-yoga-poses-for-older-adults/

Balance exercises
https://stayingsharp.aarp.org/activities/improve-balance-health/
https://www.mayoclinic.org/healthy-lifestyle/fitness/multimedia/balance-exercises/sls-20076853?s=4

https://www.mayoclinic.org/healthy-lifestyle/fitness/multimedia/balance-exercises/sls-20076853?s=2

Body mass index calculator
https://www.aarp.org/health/healthy-living/info-2017/bmi_calculator.html

Yoga for beginners
https://yogawithadriene.com/10-minute-yoga-for-beginners/
https://www.youtube.com/watch?v=v7AYKMP6rOE

simple morning stretch routine
https://www.youtube.com/watch?v=7iBm75B7LeI&t=19s

Restorative yoga stretches
https://bodybyyoga.training/yoga-for-weight-loss/restorative-yoga-stretches/
www.psychologytoday.com/us/basics/self-talk

Dealing with loneliness
www.psychologytoday.com/us/basics/loneliness

Mindfulness
https://www.psychologytoday.com/us/basics/mindfulness

Beautiful Music
www.youtube.com/watch?v=_kT38XB1YH0

Piano Music & Soft Rain
Soundwww.youtube.com/watch?v=Lp6XlsBm_Lw

3 Hour Relaxing Guitar Music: Meditation Music
www.youtube.com/watch?v=ss7EJ-PW2Uk

Self kindness
www.psychologytoday.com/us/basics/self-talk

Overcoming loneliness
www.psychologytoday.com/us/basics/loneliness

Avoiding dependence on your cell phone
www.psychologytoday.com/us/blog/click-here-
happiness/201806/are-you-phone-addict

Avoiding dependence on your cell phone
https://www.psychologytoday.com/us/basics/mindfulness

Reducing depression
https://www.psychologytoday.com/us/basics/depression

Chocolate
www.sciencedaily.com/releases/2007/09/070911073921.htm
www.science.org.au/curious/everything-else/chocolate
https://pubmed.ncbi.nlm.nih.gov/11363932/
www.sciencedaily.com/releases/2007/02/070221101326.htm
https://bebrainfit.com/brain-foods

Metronome light
www.menshealth.com/technology-gear/g23397130/best-
sleep-tech/

Fragrant oils to aid sleep
https://www.youngliving.com/blog/oils-for-sleep

Oldies tunes https://renewmusic.com/channels

Games and quizzes
www.merriam-webster.com/games

Turn an online friend into a friend in real life
https://www.meetup.com/blog/how-to-turn-an-online-
connection-into-an-irl-friend/

Investing in friendships
psychologytoday.com/us/contributors/allison-e-mcwilliams-phd

Effects and risks of alcohol
www.nytimes.com/2023/01/13/well/mind/alcohol-health-effects.html
www.washingtonpost.com/wellness/2023/03/31/moderate-drinking-alcohol-wine-risks/
www.bloomberg.com/news/articles/2022-01-20/is-a-glass-of-wine-a-day-good-for-me-heart-federation-says-no

Gardening: https://local.aarp.org/gardening/events [AARP]

Basics of woodcarving
www.youtube.com/watch?v=axiGtO48_KE

Senior living sites
www.aplaceformom.com/best-of-senior-living-award

Calculate how much money you'll need in retirement
https://www.aarp.org/membership/benefits/finance/retirement-calculator/

Jobs for seniors   See pp. 158-159

Free cash from online activities
https://www.inboxdollars.com/

Wills: www.willmaker.com, www.legalzoom.com, eforms.com/wills, freewill.com, legalcontracts.com, doityourselfdocuments.com (also estate planning)

Senior discount newsletter seniordiscountsclub.com

Businesses offering senior discounts See p. 176

Planner for last wishes and instructions
fcaaz.org/slider-3/before-i-go-you-should-know/

Printed in Great Britain
by Amazon

45134372R00109